A COMMUNITY MANIFESTO

CHRIS WRIGHT

Earthscan Publications Ltd, London and Sterling, VA

First published in the UK and USA in 2000 by
Earthscan Publications Ltd

A catalogue record for this book is available from the
British Library

ISBN: 1 85383 734 2 paperback
        1 85383 733 4 hardback

Typesetting by JS Typesetting, Wellingborough, Northants
Printed and bound by Creative Print and Design (Wales), Ebbw Vale
Cover design by Richard Reid

For a full list of publications please contact:

Earthscan Publications Ltd
120 Pentonville Road
London, N1 9JN, UK
Tel: +44 (0)20 7278 0433
Fax: +44 (0)20 7278 1142
Email: earthinfo@earthscan.co.uk
http://www.earthscan.co.uk

22883 Quicksilver Drive, Sterling, VA 20166–2012, USA

Earthscan is an editorially independent subsidiary of Kogan Page
Ltd and publishes in association with WWF-UK and the International
Institute for Environment and Development

This book is printed on elemental chlorine-free paper

Contents

Acknowledgements v

Introduction: The Spectre of Doubt 1

A Thoroughly Modern Way of Living 5

The Fragility of the Global Money Economy 6
The Fragility of Agribusiness 13
The Fragility of Our Command-and-Control
Decision-Making Processes 20
The Fragility of the Cult of the Individual 28
Summary 37

Ways of the World 41

The Language of Life 41
Who Do We Think We Are? 54
Doing It Our Way 57
Coming to Terms with Our Unconscious 60
Enter the Scientific Viewpoint 65
So Which Way Are We Headed? 70
If You Believe That, You'll Believe Anything 73
The Paradoxical View of Life 75
Back to Basics 78
The Uncertainty Principle 83
Summary 90

Regaining a Sense of Direction 95

The Strength of Personal Responsibility 98
The Strength of Consensus 109
The Strength of Local Economies 125
The Strength of Community 141
The Wider Perspective 149
Summary 155
End Piece 159

Focusing the Mind 163

Notes and References 171

Index 175

Acknowledgements

A Community Manifesto was conceived following a LETS-LINK conference held in Portsmouth during October 1998. The subject of the two days had been complementary currencies, but speaker after speaker concentrated on the mainstream economy and its essential fragility. Perhaps we were all in the grip of millennial fever, but the feeling of approaching catastrophe was palpable. I came away with a sense that the dividing line between ourselves and the meltdown of the Russian economy or a Kosovo-style conflict was extremely thin. There is no god-given right to continuing prosperity and stability. Indeed, all the indications are that what pass for wealth and permanence today are illusory. Worse still, they are illusions that are being bought at the expense of future generations. This is simply not sustainable.

The more I thought about it, the more the storm clouds seemed to be massing in every direction. My long-held belief in the power of community to transform our world asserted itself and gave me no peace until I had completed a journey that took me from the world we take so much for granted to the more human and humane society that we must begin to build, both for our own sake and that of the generations to come.

My thanks go to Mary and Becky for their support during the writing of this book, and to Andrew Brunt and Julie Allbeson for the advice they gave at key moments during its genesis.

Introduction: The Spectre of Doubt

We live in uncertain times. Whether future generations dismiss our concerns as *fin de siècle*/millennium fever, or see us as facing up to real problems, there is a feeling abroad that crisis is just around the corner. That sense of imminent catastrophe is the more intense for the sheer number of candidates apparently queuing up to provide the *coup de grâce*. Wherever you look, the thunder clouds are massing: the meltdown of the world economy, species' extinctions, environmental degradation, decimation of the rain forest, reducing reserves of hydrocarbons, depletion of the ozone layer, overpopulation, drug-resistant superbugs, storage of nuclear waste, global warming – the list goes on and on. Our civilization has rarely felt so fragile.

There is a way of looking at history that sees the rise and fall of civilizations as a function of the way they respond, or fail to respond, to the challenges that face them. From the mists of time to the present day, one civilization after another has collapsed, some spectacularly, others with a more gradual, if apparently inevitable, decline. As far as we in the Western world are concerned – one of the few surviving representatives of the species – perhaps the best that can be said as we enter a new millennium is that the jury is still out. As Arthur Miller puts it in *The American Clock* – his play about the American experience of the Depression – 'There's never been a society that hasn't had a clock running on it'.[1]

Is such a pattern of rise and fall inevitable? In one sense the model – and it is only a model, as useful and relevant as the insights it provides – is attractive because it mirrors our own experience as individuals. Birth, death, growth, illness, hope and despair can all be detected in the descriptions of how actual civilizations have fared. There is a time for living and a time for dying and no reason to suppose that the social constructs we humans raise in order to make sense of, and shelter from, reality should be any different. No individual organism is immortal. Some trees live for many hundreds of years, but none go on forever. Death is nature's way of getting rid of the clutter that accumulates over time, allowing room for young, vigorous growth to test itself.

Clearly, societies outlive the individuals who comprise them at any one time and, in so doing, have the potential to shape and limit the options of generations yet unborn. Just as the human body is an evolutionary response to a particular set of environmental circumstances, so a culture can be seen as a response to the social problems that our being human throws up – problems that are essentially common to humanity in both time and space. Some adaptations are simply more successful than others. Looked at in this light, the history of civilizations could be seen as humanity's laboratory, experimenting with different combinations of the same basic elements to derive structures that are ever more adaptable to the circumstances we find ourselves in – evolution, in other words, on a grand scale.

The drawback of this analysis is that death is still inevitable but, as with our individual lives, it is a fact that has to be faced. Once we fail to stand up to the issues that confront us, either as individuals or cultures, we are already beginning to die. The paradox is that, as individuals, we are not very good at judging such matters. We can both feel supremely alive when gripped with a terminal illness and believe ourselves to be mortally ill when, in fact, we are in the pink. Judging our social health can be just as difficult – especially when we are on the inside.

One starting point is to recognize that if we are to overcome the difficulties that face any civilization there are at least three conditions that have to be met. Firstly, the immediate challenge should not be too great. No amount of commitment, resourcefulness or hard cash could have saved Pompeii. It was literally overwhelmed. The Armageddon scenarios that depict the earth confronted by a massive asteroid would similarly be beyond our current capacity to respond.

Secondly, the culture must possess sufficient human and material resources. The collapse of an internally weakened Roman Empire was hastened by the wave upon wave of external invasion, an unremitting tide that effectively swamped the Empire's most potent weapon – assimilation, the drawing of the 'barbarian' into the fold of the Pax Romana. Similarly, any failure to feed a population can lead to the kind of internal strife that tears a society apart from within.

Finally, and most importantly, the civilization must have the will-power, energy and vision to see what is wrong, decide what needs to be done and then to act decisively. The gradual improvement in public health in Victorian Britain – a reflection of the vigour being displayed on many fronts – gave the British Empire a new lease of life. By contrast, the David and Goliath struggle between an underdeveloped North Vietnam and the military machine of the United States showed the limitations of technology when not backed by total commitment – a realization that reverberates to this day, forming part of every dictator's thinking when confronting the emerging world order.

A brief overview of our current situation suggests that, while we face many challenges, none appears insurmountable. Likewise, we would appear to possess more human and material resources than at any time in recorded history. So, if we are to continue as a civilization, the issue is whether we have sufficient vision and will-power to survive. It does not guarantee that we will, but at least it means that the answers lie within ourselves. We can respond or not – the choice is ours. That is an awesome but liberating responsibility.

Whether we have the determination to overcome the obstacles that face us is another of those imponderables that only history will judge. Without the benefit of such hindsight we have to act in the present and those actions need to be considered, based on an understanding of the dangers and the possible options for countering them. However keyed up we may be, if we cannot see our enemies and have no strategy to deal with their likely line of advance, any response is likely to be less than effective. Put another way, while we are heroically tilting at windmills, the real threat may simply tap us on the shoulder and, before we are fully aware of what is happening, carry all before it. We need to choose our targets carefully and to be very clear about the threats they pose before we can begin to formulate an appropriate response.

A Thoroughly Modern Way of Living

There are undoubtedly many ways to view current experience, many ways to divide and subdivide its myriad facets, each allowing different points to be made and conclusions to be drawn; and, of course, none of them will come close to reflecting the complexity of the reality they are trying to describe. In this chapter, four themes are discussed that are a small part of the wider picture, namely: the fragility of the global money economy; the fragility of agribusiness; the fragility of our command-and-control decision-making processes; and the fragility of the cult of the individual. They are chosen not because they in any way define contemporary life, but because the diversity of their perspectives combines to suggest that there is a clear direction to the way that society is moving and it is a direction that is likely to increase the chance of a catastrophe overtaking our civilization rather than reducing it.

This book is about the steps we must take to minimize that risk rather than a detailed diagnosis of current problems. Having said that, some indication of the issues facing us is necessary if we are to understand the kinds of action that will be needed to mitigate them. The intention of this first chapter is to convey an impression of the forces confronting us, to produce thumb-nail sketches rather than completed works, and it is hoped that the inevitable loss of detail will be more than compensated for by the vitality and immediacy of the brushwork.

Not all the strands within each topic point in the same direction and it is always possible to produce examples that seem to contradict the general conclusion. Some trends appear to be fighting strong and successful rearguard actions or aiming for different outcomes altogether. Nevertheless, it can be argued that sufficient coherence exists both within each theme, and between them, to suggest that there are clear tendencies that we must take into account if we are to make successful adaptations to the increasingly hostile environment we find ourselves in.

THE FRAGILITY OF THE GLOBAL MONEY ECONOMY

The global economy has been likened to a supertanker with no rudder: an unstoppable force that will sink anything crossing its path. Despite some tentative steps towards a global financial framework, it is now generally acknowledged that no government or institution has control of the worldwide web of instantaneous transactions. Twenty-four hours a day, seven days a week, huge amounts of money chase the maximum return, irrespective of the social and personal consequences of the decisions that are being made. As we have seen in Asia, confidence can evaporate overnight. One day there can be an apparently healthy and growing economy and the next there is crisis that effectively consigns whole peoples to destitution.

A striking example of how the money economy has taken on a life of its own can be found in the international money markets. Currency speculation is nothing new; tourists, among others, have always had half an eye on buying and selling their money in favourable circumstances. Nevertheless, even 30 years ago, the majority of currency transactions (80–90 per cent) reflected the passage of goods and services between nations.[1] Today, only 2 per cent of a much greater volume of trading can be linked directly to the real world of trade. In other words, almost 98 per cent of all foreign exchange is estimated to be entirely speculative in nature – basically, people and institutions betting on the relative strength of one currency versus another.

It is not hard to see how weak currencies can be sent to the wall almost on a whim, nor why one of the strongest arguments for developments such as the euro is the greater protection it can offer against the speculator. The perceived strength of the dollar has long been based on the fact that there is so much of the stuff (California, for example, is the seventh largest economy in the world in its own right). Even when times were hard in America, it offered a safer haven than most.

And it is not just the currency markets. The trend towards increasing speculation is reflected in all aspects of the global economy – from stock markets to futures, derivatives and hedge funds. The world of money has ceased to connect with everyday experience or correspond to the social value that is to be found in real goods and services. Instead it is played according to rules that owe more to professional gambling than to normal human intercourse. But, unlike a casino, there is no central institution as arbiter and ultimate beneficiary, only the gamblers endlessly competing with each other. The stakes get bigger and bigger, and the risks taken get ever greater.

The green economist, James Robertson,[2] has likened the operation of the global money economy to the Roman Catholic Church in medieval times, when the buying and selling of indulgences had become an end in itself – a way to generate fabulous wealth and influence for the priesthood rather than the means by which the faithful could receive absolution in this life or, more importantly, in the next. In both cases, corruption and greed were the natural outcome of processes that are nothing more than simple human exchange. It took the Reformation to purge the Church of its excesses.

Even if the world economy continues to lurch from one crisis to another without crashing (in other words, the speculators, like ivy, manage to bleed the system without actually killing it), the sheer size and increasing volatility of the markets is having an ever greater effect on what individual governments can do in their own backyard. The kind of tight fiscal controls that have traditionally been imposed by the International Monetary Fund as part of any restructuring of the debt that besets most developing nations have now become part and parcel of the economic scene in the industrialized world.

They are essentially blunt instruments – interest rates, taxation, reducing public sector borrowing by cutting public services – but failure to keep one's economic house in order risks speculators putting pressure on a currency, pressure that no national government can now resist on its own. Improving public services, greater democracy, increased social inclusion or a redistribution of wealth through taxation – some of the real issues governments are elected to tackle – have become very secondary considerations when set against the need to manage, and be seen to manage, a sound economy. The key institutional measures of how an economy is performing have come to far outweigh the needs of individual human beings. The omens for democracy are not good.

This increasingly narrow emphasis on financial probity has several consequences. Because the instruments are blunt they can have wildly different effects on different groups of people and different parts of the country. Raising interest rates may have a neutral effect on business in London, with its emphasis on financial services, but may be disastrous for small entrepreneurs on Merseyside. A drop in petrol prices can be good news for consumers and manufacturers while, at the same time and within the same country, causing redundancy and a tightening of belts in those areas that are dependent on the oil industry.

In making his now infamous quote about the loss of jobs in the North East of England being an acceptable price to pay for maintaining low inflation, Eddie George, the Governor of the Bank of England, was only telling the truth. Keeping that limited range of economic indicators stable will always be the priority in keeping speculation at bay, no matter what the consequences. The problem is that jobs, once lost, cannot be recreated. No amount of resources redirected, after the event, through grants, regional aid and so on, can repair the damage that arbitrary changes in the macroeconomy cause.

So what is new? Human experience has always been about winners and losers. Possibly, but we are talking here about whole communities, even nations, sidelined because of a need to respond to the perceived threat of speculation. As we move to supranational currencies, such as the euro, the problem will only get worse. The capitalism of Karl Marx was about the appropriation of the fruit of the workers' toil in the form of profit. We have entered a post-capitalist era in which the everyday lives of real people across the globe are being staked in a game that bears less and less resemblance to either toil or fruit.

The speculator is essentially interested in the greatest gain in the shortest time, which is why there has been a surge in high risks such as junk bonds and hedging. This preoccupation is now mirrored in the attitudes of individuals, companies and nations who habitually seek out the best short-term deal – which is usually defined as the

cheapest option for a given level of quality – without thinking of the long-term consequences either to the purchaser
(in terms of energy consumption, sustainability, and so on)
or the provider (in terms of the conditions in which the
product was made). Ethical trading is a niche market
that has more to do with providing a feel-good factor than
changing the world order.

The whole system is built on an elaborate structure of
loans. We have all heard of Third World Debt but the largest
debtors are, in fact, the richest countries (led by the United
States, with an estimated $5000 billion of personal debt).[3]
The biggest lenders are the multinational banks and financial institutions, and recent mergers demonstrate that huge
corporations are being formed to service lending on an ever
greater scale. Banks compete with each other to extend
credit and, in the process, to create money (an estimated
95 per cent of all money is created in this way)[4] which then
chases a return – in terms of goods and services or, more
likely, further investment/speculation.

It is a house built on sand, a sleight of hand that works
(and then only according to its own distorted logic) as long
as the global economy continues to expand. A hint of con-
traction in any part of the system – or, worse still, in the
whole – leads to speculators seeking to liquidize their assets
for reinvestment elsewhere. This combination of events
provokes the banks to recall loans and restrict future credit.
A restriction of credit makes it more difficult for large-scale
debtors, such as manufacturers, to create the additional
wealth to repay their loans, which in turn produces job
losses, bankruptcies and a knock-on effect on individuals
who can no longer service their own, more modest debts,
leading to house repossession, and so on. It is the classic
case of a slump and it is entirely the product of an unstable
monetary system. In other words, it does not reflect reality

on the ground. Communities where money was once freely available find that it has suddenly vanished – gone elsewhere in pursuit of greater returns – affecting the quality of life of all concerned.

Money is like an all-purpose lubricant. Without it the engine of daily life seizes up and stops moving. The people within the community have not changed, nor the skills and energy that are available, only their relative competitiveness in the global economy. The consequence is that people find it increasingly difficult to meet the needs they once took for granted. In his book *Short Circuit*,[5] Richard Douthwaite shows how a community can cease to be viable simply because it no longer has anything to contribute to the mainstream economy – a circumstance made inevitable by decisions taken in far-distant boardrooms on the basis of priorities that have nothing to do with sustaining communities that may have existed for centuries.

Although debt fuels the engines of growth in the short term, it can also have long-term consequences for generations to come. In *The Pity of War*,[6] for example, Niall Ferguson estimates that during the First World War public debt in Britain rose by a factor of ten and provided a drain on the national exchequer until the 1960s. Rather closer to home, that model of cradle-to-grave welfare, Sweden, has reached the stage where national debt is almost equal to the annual gross domestic product and 7 per cent of production goes just to service it.

The situation in many developing nations is even more dire, with whole economies in hock to their creditors – people in other countries (mainly the Western world) creaming off the wealth produced by local people and, in doing so, denying them access to even basic social and health-care programmes. Anyone with a mortgage will be familiar with the basic mechanism, paying several times the value of an asset because one lacked the resources (capital) to buy it outright. 'For the person who has will always be given more, till they have enough and to spare; and the person who has not will forfeit even what they have' (Matthew 25:29). Nothing changes.

It also goes without saying that the people with money are not actually the people who need it most in terms of their ability to live a halfway decent life. When times are difficult it will be the poor who suffer the most. It was always thus, but the vagaries of the global economy outlined above (which, it cannot be stressed too often, is operated for no other purpose than to make money on the game of the day for those who happen to have it at the moment) will only make the swings in the pendulum even more erratic. And because the cumulative and destabilizing social effects of such cycles on towns, regions and whole nations will cause real pain, there is likely to be an increase in social disorder.

It is salutary to remember that it took the Second World War to end the Great Depression and that Japan became a leading economy on the back of the Korean War. In *Nineteen Eighty-Four*,[7] George Orwell anticipated a world dominated by three superpowers in a state of continual war. Little territory was ever gained, but economies on a war footing were stable and the populations were controlled by a mixture of propaganda and fear. War is good for business and has certain political attractions. It may yet be the only way out of the economic mire into which we seem to be rushing.

Of course, if the whole system crashes (and many observers believe there is an evens chance of a global meltdown within the first decade of the 21st century) the result could be the end of civilization as we know it.

THE FRAGILITY OF AGRIBUSINESS

Any society ultimately depends on its stomach being full. To create for the long term, to invest in the future, requires confidence that our hopes might be realized. Many factors contribute to that belief, but among the most fundamental is knowing where one's next meal is coming from. That may seem a superfluous, even flippant, observation when we look at supermarket shelves groaning with produce from the four corners of the world. We have had butter and beef mountains and wine lakes. Surely the problem is over-production, not the reverse?

In one sense that is true. The industrialized world is capable of producing consistent surpluses of food and is rich enough to import the staples and more exotic produce to ensure that its citizens can buy anything (provided they have the money), all the year round – the very seasons themselves have been defeated. The rest of the world is not so fortunate, and to realize that all is not well closer to home we have only to look at the plight of the small farmer.

Over large parts of Europe small farmers are being forced to sell up – in many cases after generations of farming the same piece of land – because they can no longer make ends meet. The problem is that for each category of farming and in each country there is a different immediate cause for the crisis. For some it is the strength of the national currency which encourages a flood of cheap imports, for others it is fashion or superior marketing or the unintended outcome of national or international policies. A drop in public confidence following a health scare can mean the difference between survival and going bust while, for yet others, it may be that small-scale farming is just no longer financially viable.

13

Common to all, however, is a switch from seeing the land as a legacy to be nurtured for both current consumption and future use, to exploiting it as a business. And business is about gaining the competitive edge through innovation and mechanization that pushes up productivity and pushes down prices. Its concerns are short term.

That transformation has not occurred overnight. It has gone hand in hand with the increasing mechanization of farming methods (implying the need for ever greater capital investment), but it has been speeded up by the trends outlined above in the global economy as a whole. Farms of all sizes are in debt to the banks, and banks are interested in only one thing – getting a return on their money. They may not wish to see farmers go under, but their definition of the point at which they demand their assets because it is no longer economically viable for them to continue is a narrow one – namely, the health of the balance sheet.

When times are hard farmers traditionally pull in their horns and wait for things to improve. They can at least provide for their own needs. That option is no longer available because others, who have no interest in farming per se, are in control and farmers' wealth, as defined in monetary terms, lies in their land, buildings and equipment, not in what they use them for. Hence, there is no alternative to selling up. It is the small farmers who are least fitted to riding out the ups and down of market forces (which may be created by factors that are essentially non-economic, such as the Common Agricultural Policy) and, not surprisingly, they are the ones who are going to the wall first.

Would it be a tragedy if the small farmer became a thing of the past? We all have to move with the times, and if the only way to make farming pay is to operate bigger and bigger units then what is the problem? The logic of agribusiness is certainly towards greater productivity and

14

efficiency, and the technology that can deliver these ultimately requires increasing scale for both technical reasons
(bigger machines cope better on larger, regular fields) and
financial ones (a unit of capital is more easily absorbed by
a larger operation). With the growth in supermarkets and
the consequent decline in the high street greengrocer, there
has also been a squeeze on producers' margins, for which
large-scale production is the only logical response.

This trend is by no means uniform. New technology does
provide opportunities for small-scale specialization and the
cooperative use of expensive machinery at least offers the
possibility of smaller units surviving into the future. There
is also the movement towards organic farming. Overall,
however, the pressures point in one direction. There are so
many factors that can throw even the best laid plans off
course that the future favours the forms of organization that
are most able to accommodate them. Size has obvious
advantages and, in the long run, profit follows the line of
least resistance.

Technology is also seductive. The latest generation of
combine harvesters are state-of-the-art machines, combin-
ing computer technology with ease of operation. At the flick
of a switch, the driver, sitting in air-conditioned comfort,
can set the rotors for any crop. Each machine costs well in
excess of the cost of an average house. To complement such
sophistication, farmers can now rely on satellite technology
to tell them what to plant, the optimum time to plant it
and when to harvest. Information scanned each time a
satellite passes overhead is fed into a central computer that
compares the data with what has happened in the past,
both on that land and elsewhere, and makes predictions
about the yield over a range of options. It can even identify
a section of land where growth is delayed for some reason,
allowing the farmer to programme the computer on the

tractor's hoppers to deliver more fertilizer to that area as the field is traversed.

It is a technological miracle but it is dangerous for several reasons. Firstly, the greater the injection of technology, the larger farms are likely to become, and the larger they become the more likely it is that they will be owned by corporations with a range of interests, including the sale of fertilizers and farm machinery. The land will come to be seen as something to be bought and sold like any other commodity. Such ownership at a distance will mean employing farm managers who will also have no long-term investment in the land because their performance is judged by what they deliver in the here and now.

Secondly, farming has always been an unpredictable activity. Climate and weather are hard taskmasters and success has never come easily. A farmer uses his knowledge, experience and feel for a piece of land to make the key decisions. It is essentially a holistic approach to complex experience, relying as much on intuition (with a dollop of luck) as a rational analysis of the information available. To become dependent on technology in the way described above is to reverse a centuries-old relationship, which has been as much about learning to work with the grain of nature as it has been about growing food. Humankind's attempts to connect with the world out there is an elemental dance and to lose that primordial dimension is to sever the last, tenuous link that we have with the physical environment that nurtures and sustains us.

If that sounds overly romantic, it is worth reflecting that small-scale farming is both a hard life and one that runs counter to much of the kind of kindergarden imagery (largely urban-based) that characterizes many of our perceptions about animal welfare. It is a way of life that provides direct experience of nature and a continuity with past generations who engaged in the same struggles. Once that has gone, we will have become totally divorced from our ecosystem and will have finally lost the ability to discern the messages that nature gives us about what we are doing to the planet.

Thirdly, gargantuan farming operations will tend inevitably towards a monoculture with all the dangers that come with a narrowing of diversity. Mixed farming is a small-scale, self-sustaining, natural system, rotating crops and recycling manure and other waste, and is likely to be relatively hardy and resistant to external change. By contrast, large areas of single crops or animals are less resistant to the introduction of pests or disease. As a consequence, such farms will be more dependent on chemical defences as a matter of course, implying the routine inoculation of livestock and the spraying of crops.

Without even being aware of it, we have been moving ever further from a concept of farming as being about producing healthy foodstuffs to one in which the emphasis is on suppressing the lack of health that comes from applying the techniques of the factory to agriculture: without the low levels of antibiotics being fed to cattle and hens throughout their lives – which also promote a small weight gain – disease would wipe out animals that are kept in over-crowded conditions; without the regular applications of herbicides, cereals that are grown year after year on the same fields – that is, without rotation – would be choked by super weeds. There are now signs that the bacteria that are essential to productivity are declining on fields that have become heavily dependent on artificial fertilizers – the soil itself is becoming sterile.

Such conglomerates, with power residing in some distant boardroom, are also much more likely to approve intensive farming methods, genetically modified crop varieties and the introduction of risky techniques (such as the contamination of cattle feed that many people believe initiated the BSE (bovine spongiform encephalopathy) crisis) because they appear to offer better financial returns. Farming is a conservative business, but the bigger the operation the faster innovations of all kinds, both positive and negative, will be introduced and the bigger the potential disasters are likely to be as a consequence.

The greatest threat to agribusiness farming, however, has nothing to do with the size of farm, technology or available capital. At the end of the day the whole system depends on one element – fossil fuels in the form of hydrocarbons – and it is going to be in short supply in the very near future – 20 or 30 years into the new millennium, according to even conservative sources.[8] Unless major technological change is forthcoming on a global scale, most of the high-tech equipment on which modern agriculture depends will grind to a halt.

The processes by which food is prepared for, and transported to, the table will likewise begin to fail. And, worst of all, the chemical fixes (in the form of fertilizers, pesticides, cattle feeds, and so on) to which farming has become addicted and without which the growth in the yields needed to feed increasing expectations (including obesity) will be a thing of the past. No amount of managerial expertise can compensate for deficits like that. Inputs and outputs will slump. The system will cease to function. And it is not just agribusiness that will be effected by a shortage of oil, but our whole way of living.

One of the threads that links the collapse of earlier civilizations has been the presence of perverse incentives in the wider economy that have pushed farmers to overexploit their land or otherwise led to a loss of sustainability in the long term. Deserts can be the result of long-term climatic changes; they can also represent the point at which the demand for food from growing cities overwhelmed their hinterlands.

The Common Agricultural Policy, acting with the same arbitrariness as interest rates on the wider business community, has distorted the way in which food has been produced in Europe for decades and, by ushering in the state of affairs we now see, may have dealt agriculture a mortal blow. Even more telling is the way in which farmers in the developing world have been encouraged to switch from self-sufficiency to the production of cash crops. In many cases this economically desirable development (it boosts the gross domestic product of the countries concerned, earns foreign currency and produces a profit for the shippers and middlemen) has resulted in farmers sinking ever deeper into debt and having to overwork the land in a desperate attempt to keep their heads above water.

Production begins to tail off as land is overutilized, more fertilizers are needed and debt increases. Because land is devoted to cash crops, the farmers can no longer produce enough to feed their own families; they now have to buy food and their debt increases yet further. It is a vicious circle that only ends when the farmer is forced off the land, to be replaced by more 'efficient' methods that are dependent on increasing (imported) technological fixes and the ever bigger units that are needed to be financially viable. One more family ceases to be self-sufficient and instead becomes an entry in the statistics of the urban poor.

It is always easy to see the trends after the event, to see in the wastelands the folly of the people who created them. Foresight is more difficult, but it is not hard to conclude that, even without the hydrocarbon crisis looming on the horizon, the increasingly large-scale nature of agriculture – determined by its economic efficiency – is unlikely to be sustainable in the long term. Farmers are already having to run to keep up and that is a recipe for overexploitation of the land and its gradual degradation as a result. Without a healthy agricultural base, no civilization has a long-term future.

THE FRAGILITY OF OUR COMMAND-AND-CONTROL DECISION-MAKING PROCESSES

Command-and-control decision-making processes imply a high degree of centralization. They are linked indelibly to the arthritic state structures that characterized the economy of the Soviet Union before its collapse. In the sense that it is used here, however, the phrase is simply shorthand for taking decisions at a distance from the point at which they have their impact. The greater the distance between the two, and the more filters or channels the decision has to pass through to reach its destination, the greater is the degree of command and control. In its ultimate form the recipients of the decision/order have to respond in a stylized, predictable way that permits little or no freedom of interpretation or action (except in so far as the 'Chinese whispers' nature of its transmission allows for a distortion of the message along the way which, people being people, will be seized upon and exploited).

The essentially top-down nature of the process is evident in the way that governments operate. It is evident too in the large-scale institutions that dominate the social and economic landscape such as law, medicine, banking and education. By their very nature these are the aspects of social reality that require and promote order and stability. The organizational response to providing this order has been typically bureaucratic, with a high premium placed on accountability, predictability, precedent, fairness and, above all, rationality. Such structures are hierarchical, conservative by nature and dominated by rules. They are classic command and control.

Social Security is an example of a bureaucracy at work. Who is eligible and how much they will receive is defined carefully centrally and great effort is expended in trying to ensure that these 'rules' are applied consistently across the many offices where claimants can register. From application, through assessment to possible appeal, the emphasis is on squeezing the myriad personal circumstances into categories that simply either permit payment or exclude it.

The process is its own justification and the sizeable appeal industry that has grown up focuses on how it has been applied rather than on any notion of the intrinsic merit of a case (even down to advising on the appropriate use of language to maximize the chances of success). It is morally deaf and blind, producing endless statistics about applications processed, awards made, appeals heard, and so on to show the amount of work that has been shifted as a way of avoiding the difficult questions about what the system is trying to achieve. As a consequence, opinion becomes polarized between those who think all applicants are scroungers and dependants, and others who believe that a basic wage should be available to all.

Such organizations are closed systems whose strength is their ability to repeat the same operations over and over again accurately and effectively. In that sense they are like machines, and machines are incapable of transforming themselves if needs change. They have to be re-engineered, which is costly and time consuming. In the same way, bureaucracies are notoriously difficult to reform and, beyond a certain level of tinkering, can cease to function at all.

Max Weber, who first outlined its key features, foresaw that bureaucracy's very efficiency would sweep all before it in any large-scale society because it offered a decision-making process that could deal effectively with large numbers of people without the need for physical force. Much as he admired the sheer competence of the bureaucratic model, he also deplored its impact on the human spirit because, at the end of the day, order and stability are only one side of human nature. Although we undoubtedly require a degree of security and predictability to function effectively (which has to be provided in a social context – that is, we cannot achieve it as isolated individuals), we also respond to the ability (actual or perceived) to make our own choices and decisions, to take risks and to develop as unique beings. In short, there is a balance between order and freedom, between predictability and change and between safety and danger and, in a bureaucracy, that balance is all one way.

Society has altered out of all recognition in the last hundred years and only one thing seems certain – that everything will continue to change. That experience of remorseless and ever faster change has obvious consequences for organizations that are only good at standing still. Thirty years ago Alvin Toffler predicted in his book *Future Shock*[9] that we were witnessing the breakdown of bureaucracy and its replacement by new kinetic, fluid structures that would come into being and disappear again in accordance with changing circumstances. The ever increasing speed of change would favour those loosely knit groups that could adapt their structures and relationships to respond.

Organizations, in so far as they existed, would be self-renewing, bolting on new bits and disposing of the old, and traditional hierarchies would be replaced by shifting networks of lateral relationships that emphasized utility to the task in hand rather than position. Cooperation would be at least as important as competition in facing the challenges of the future. Toffler offered an organic image for organizations rather than a mechanistic one.

It remains a perceptive, not to say seductive, analysis and much of what Toffler foresaw has come to pass. Nothing today is forever. Our commitment to people, places and things is more transient than before, we are obsessed with novelty and are superficially more tolerant of difference and letting people do their own thing. Society has loosened up and these changes have all had an impact on the organizations that form the daily backdrop for most people. Employees think in terms of personal career rather than loyalty to any one idea or employer. Companies have fewer qualms about offloading staff who are not flexible enough to respond to changing needs or axing whole sections in the wake of restructuring, downsizing or cost-cutting exercises. The pursuit of profit has become the universal measure of success.

For those in work the pressures are increasing. It is ironic that in a time of continuing unemployment people are again having to work longer and longer hours, sacrificing home and family to stay in the game. Change is everywhere. Information technology is transforming both the skills required to be successful and the nature of the tasks to be performed. There has already been a marked shift from manufacture to the service sector. We are now witnessing a further shift into what might be called the virtual world of information. Cyberspace has opened up an (as far as we know) unlimited marketplace and the growth in exploiting it remains exponential.

Companies are having to adapt and readapt. The monolithic structures that used to offer a job for life have gone the way of the dinosaur, to be replaced by slimmed-down core activities supported by an increasing number of contracted out services (from information technology to transportation). Rather than a vertically integrated hierarchy, the picture is more of a spider's web with burgeoning links between the centre (the corporate task) and the periphery (the suppliers – located, increasingly, on different continents).

All these trends are pushing organizations in the ways that Alvin Toffler described. And yet the corporate world remains as rigidly controlled and internally competitive as ever. It is as if external pressures have been trying to push the flesh into radically different shapes while, underneath, the skeleton has remained essentially unaltered. On the surface it is all speed, glitter and excitement but, fundamentally, the framework of command and control continues unchanged.

Bone structure (its size, shape, strength, and so on) will always determine the ultimate shape of the body and the limits of its adaptability. It is probable that, even if skeletons could alter more rapidly, the animal that emerged at the end of the day would still have only changed its spots. Greater and more rapid change is a two-edged sword, especially in a culture where individual rights are emphasized. Alongside the demand for creativity and adaptability can be ranged the surge in rules and regulations covering areas such as employment law, health and safety at work, equal opportunities and the increasingly active consumer rights movement. At heart this emphasis on the rights of individuals as against those of organizations is legalistic and, as we have seen, the law is one of those areas of society that seeks order through command-and-control structures.

Although at first glance the law might be considered infinite in its scope (and therefore infinitely flexible), with very little that can escape its net, it is actually amazingly pedestrian in its execution. The law operates through precedent (the use of previous judgements – case law – to weigh current suits in the balance), and precedent is ultimately tested in the highest court in the land. It is thus a hierarchical framework of judgments that seeks to be internally consistent and to be administered in a rational and reasonable way in many different settings. As with any command-and-control structure, it will work well only if two preconditions are met: firstly, the initial objective must be sound – that is, the legal base must be sensible – and change must not happen too quickly.

In a fast-moving society, neither of those conditions is met, which leads to absurdities where ancient precedent is quoted to decide cases that bear no comparison. When new employment law is introduced, for example, no one knows what the full implications will be and companies await the setting of precedent and hope that it will not be them in the dock. Good intent and reasonableness are no defence and, as a consequence, an organization's posture will be defensive, on the one hand instinctively reacting against the attempt to limit a sphere of action, and on the other seeking to pay lip-service to the new regulations by introducing policies that will protect against the loose cannon or bad luck.

In small groupings where people know each other it is relatively easy to gauge the responses of employees. But, as companies increase in size, so does their exposure both in terms of the risk that something will go wrong and also in terms of the way that any court might view their need to act responsibly – that is, to be seen to implement the regulations.

Because the process is at heart legalistic and will be tested ultimately in a legal setting, there is a tendency to employ lawyers and other experts who will look at the issues from a legal point of view, drafting contracts with suppliers and framing policy in a way that will offer maximum protection if challenged. This need to safeguard against potentially costly and time-consuming litigation (that most business people intuitively feel uncomfortable with) produces a centralizing tendency. When the people at the centre do not necessarily know what employees elsewhere in the organization (or its suppliers) are doing, it is likely to be asking too much of trust to allow them to develop the kind of anarchic, cellular structures proposed by Toffler.

When the environment is one in which neither employer nor employee expects or wishes to offer loyalty, the tendency is always to attempt to reassert control. It is easier to centralize than to fragment in a world where the law is the ultimate arbiter of success. As supranational states such as Europe begin to emerge, that tendency will accelerate. Rules and regulations will proliferate and going with the flow and becoming a command-and-control system yourself will be the only sensible option. Slimmed down and dispersed the new frameworks may be, but they are held together by the high tensile coils of contract as effectively as ever they were when control was visibly at the centre.

If we are stuck with command-and-control decision-making systems, why can't we make the best of a bad job? What is so very wrong with something that is, after all, very familiar? Put simply, they assume that people like you and me have no independent existence. We are all reduced to the level of statistics, categorized and labelled in simplistic, one-dimensional ways that deny both our uniqueness and our complexity. As a consequence, they permit the kind of decision-making that accepts that raising interest rates is in the national interest even if the price to pay is people in the North East losing their jobs. They allow people in need to be denied benefit because they don't fit in with the criteria laid down. They mean that people in North-ampton and Naples, Southampton and Seville will be expected to behave in broadly similar ways. In short, they deny our humanity and allow things to happen that would be inconceivable between fully feeling people.

It gets worse. By their nature, command-and-control systems try to operate on the basis that nothing is changing. In a culture where change is one of the dominant themes, such structures can appear increasingly bizarre. Many of our high-profile institutions, such as health and education, appear to be in continual crisis with one reorganization after another attempting to make them finally competitive and efficient. Morale among staff slumps ever further and service users – the customers – are faced with endlessly changing demands that they are expected to fit in with.

Because they function in an essentially top-down fashion, organizations based on command and control receive only limited feedback on the actual impact of their decisions. Boardrooms can continue to believe that all in the garden in rosy while, at the coal face, confusion, anger and a couldn't-care-less attitude are being conveyed to the customer. In nature, feedback is the primary way in which organisms perceive what is happening to them, allowing them to attempt adaptive strategies and, ultimately, to retreat. Without such a lifesaving capacity, our large, mechanistic organizations lumber around doing immense harm. People get trampled underfoot, particularly in the coils of a legal system that is theoretically there to protect their rights.

In a fragile world where threats are on every side, com-mand and control is more likely to increase the difficulties than ameliorate them. And, when all the significant levers of power are in the hands of such institutions, it is hard to see how catastrophe can be avoided in the long run. The way that the BSE crisis was handled may well represent a chilling blueprint for the future.

THE FRAGILITY OF THE CULT OF THE INDIVIDUAL

The history of the Western world since the Enlightenment can be viewed as the gradual erosion of traditional ties and obligations. Rousseau's famous dictum, 'Man is born free, and everywhere he is in chains', neatly encapsulates the push to throw off arbitrarily imposed duties and replace them with rationally defensible rights. From feudalism to patriarchy, from aristocracy to unfettered capitalism, all bastions of power based on the privilege of position have had to give ground and retreat in the face of the ongoing exploration of what it means to protect every individual on the planet from exploitation and abuse.

A milestone along this road was the 'Universal Declaration of Human Rights' accepted by the United Nations General Assembly on 10 December 1948.[10] Article 2 states that 'everyone is entitled to all the rights and freedoms set forth in this Declaration, without distinction of any kind, such as race, colour, sex, language, religion, political or other opinion, national or social origin, property, birth or other status'. They are universal rights, enshrined in law, and 'all (people) are equal before the law and are entitled without any discrimination to equal protection of the law' (Article 7). Member nations are to create 'competent national tribunals' to ensure that 'everyone has the right to an effective remedy ... for acts violating the fundamental rights granted them by the constitution or by law' (Article 8).

Violations against both the spirit and the letter of this Declaration may be commonplace in the world today, but there is a commitment among the international community to root out all such abuse. In a world that is becoming ever more transparent through the use of modern communications technology, it is easier to detect and disseminate information about infringements of human rights. Oppressed minorities can make their case on the Internet, international support can be mobilized and focused almost instantly. Such knowledge makes it easier to do something about maltreatment – or, at least, it is less easy to ignore it.

The struggle for human rights might therefore be considered won but, from the standpoint of the 21st century, will it be considered a Pyrrhic victory? There is no disputing the achievements, nor the respect that should be accorded to those who have suffered and died in the pursuit of justice. It is, however, in the nature of all inheritors to take for granted the progress that has been handed to them and to say 'so what?' as they prepare to fight the battles that seem important to them.

Those battles are likely to reflect the fact that, despite the redress that is now readily available to them, individuals today can, paradoxically, feel more endangered and more threatened with being overwhelmed by forces beyond their control than ever before, precisely because their welfare has become so dependent on a legal system that just is not delivering the goods. Faced with the power of the institutional world to remove our livelihood, to pollute our atmosphere and to damage our health in a hundred unseen ways, where are we to turn when the law looks the other way?

In the scheme of things we increasingly exist only in so far as we fit in with the criteria (conscious and unconscious) that justify the existence of such large-scale structures. Once we step outside those restricted limits, we risk finding ourselves alone and exposed. Institutional racism (whether 'intended' or not), sexism, ageism, etc, are only some of

29

the manifestations of the way that institutions discount us all as individuals.

The well-trodden route of remedying injustice through an extension or redefinition of rights is no longer working. In fact, it often makes the problem worse. We appear to have reached a dead end because pursuing civil rights has become a matter of legal, rather than moral, debate. What matters is not the 'rightness' of an issue but whether it can be upheld in legal terms.

Although there is a global debate about the need to balance rights with responsibilities, we seem to have settled for a straightforward legalistic model of redress. Where responsibility is at issue it is usually expressed in an institutional sense, as in 'it is an employer's responsibility', and reflects liability in some way. It is a very limited interpretation of 'responsibility' and, as we shall see later, the law may be ideal for coping with the minutiae of contract and determining whether a particular statute has been transgressed, but it struggles with the more open-ended nature of the responsibilities that link real people together.

The law, as already stated, is also an institutionally guided set of responses. It is not there for the individual in the way that one's family or tribe might be. Arbitrary and imbalanced they may have been, but traditional ties of kinship and feudal obligation implied a degree of reciprocity. When the chips were down, individuals could count on support from their immediate group.

By contrast, in approaching the law, the individual is always the supplicant, pleading to be allowed within its portals. There is no warmth or sense of human contact. Objectively and without feeling, the law weighs each individual's claim on its own scales and, like Social Security, only responds to predefined categories: a sense of grievance is only legally a sense of grievance in certain circumstances.

It is a potentially costly process and, with an increase in plea bargaining and out-of-court settlements (to minimize cost, the risk of 'losing' and the potential precedent that losing might create), may not even deliver what the individual is seeking.

Because the issue that is being judged is not uniquely yours or mine, but an abstraction or generalization based on a complex and arcane set of rules, it is perhaps not surprising that going to the law produces low levels of satisfaction even when one's position is apparently vindicated. The system is based on conflict, winning and losing, and participants are encouraged to go for bust. Positions are hyped up and pilloried, yet emotion – all the manifold feelings associated with having a grievance – is carefully excluded and the possibility of reconciliation is literally ruled out of court.

As such, both the concept of the law and its application are in marked contrast to the way in which ordinary individuals attempt to resolve their differences. With people we know, most of us, for most of the time, will instinctively seek a win-win solution that takes the viewpoint of both parties into consideration and allows their feelings to be ventilated and dissipated. Only in rare and exceptional circumstances does the situation degenerate into violence or the threat of violence. When it does, dangerous forces can be unleashed. Feuds are deeply ingrained in the human psyche and, while two tribes or families may quickly lose any sense of what the original injury was about, the existence of a feud at least acknowledged the feelings associated with it. Our legal system does not even begin to address such issues.

It is worth remembering that the law evolved to deal with three distinct categories of offence: those against property, those against the person and those that might be broadly classed as being against public order. Property was simply about title and, as such, was usually 'open and shut'. Divorce (available, if at all, only to the rich) fell into this category and was essentially about disentangling the parties' property (including children) according to legal precedent. Murder and other serious crimes against the person were tried and, in theory at least, the aim was to establish the truth. The person under suspicion might be required to participate in the trial by submitting themselves to torture (the ancient ritual of trial by ordeal), but the process had clearly prescribed limits and notions of fairness. Again, the issues being addressed were simple and straightforward – did the act take place and was it punishable in legal terms? Questions of competence to plead sanity or state of mind did not enter into the equation.

Matters relating to public order were usually dealt with more or less informally by the system of Justices of the Peace – squires and local dignitaries, appointed for the purpose, who knew their localities and populations and were known in return: both sides knew what to expect and, within the rules of the game, accommodations could be made to suit particular circumstances. In all three categories people at the bottom of the pile rarely got justice, in the sense that they would be treated differently from those at the top, but at least the issues were clear.

This simple and simplistic framework is now groaning under the load of the dramatic rise in the numbers entitled to seek redress through the law, the sheer breadth and volume of legislation and the increasing tendency to see the law as an option of first, rather than last, resort. The family continues to fragment (50 per cent of all marriages in the US end in divorce, with a similar figure in the UK, and 50 per cent of American children and almost 25 per cent of British children are brought up in single parent families) and the relationships within and between generations become more complex. As a result, there is less and less 'core' (stable, long-term relationships) and more and more 'surface' (superficial, short-term, role-oriented acquaintanceships) to our lives. We know fewer and fewer people well enough to take the 'human' route and, as a consequence, more and more disputes are being referred to the courts.

As local ties continue to atrophy, more and more aspects of daily life will be drawn into the legal arena as laws are passed to deal with everything from noisy neighbours to unsafe cars. Add to these developments the general advances in education and understanding, the acceptance of a more relativistic stance on moral and social issues, and it is clear that the expectations of what the legal system can deliver are totally at variance with what it can possibly achieve. The trends seem so inevitable, however, that it is hard to see where the alternative might lie.

Another perspective on the way the law is taking centre stage as a prime arbiter in human relationships is to recognize that authority (in the form of government, whether at local or national level) continues to become ever more distanced from each of us as individuals because of the size of the population and the disappearance of effective intermediate groupings such as communities. In such circumstances its only possible response to the problems it is presented with (usually media or interest group generated) is to enact new laws. Laws replace dialogue and often reflect the fact that dialogue has ceased to exist or is producing issues too complex to resolve.

The existence of such a wide-ranging legislative base leads inevitably to the rise of the 'expert', both to police the regulations and to advise on how they might be circumvented. From financial advisers to surveyors, from personal fitness consultants to environmental health inspectors, we seek to smooth the passage of our lives. Such 'expertise' is itself subject to scrutiny both in terms of an increasing willingness to sue for what is perceived to be negligent behaviour and also through public enquiries that are set up to establish responsibility and 'blame' for tragedies involving public services. The introduction of no-win/no-fee legal advice will accelerate these trends if only because solicitors know that a) the law of averages is with them – they may lose some but they will also win some – and b) insurers will often settle out of court to avoid time-consuming and costly court appearances.

Because experts have a necessarily limited viewpoint and approach each problem from a standardized, quasi-legal basis, the individual will rarely receive advice that takes him or her, as a whole person, into account. The intervention of one profession may create problems that require another to become involved. Quite often the requirements laid down to comply with the regulations of different agencies are contradictory: follow one and you get into trouble with the other, and vice versa. It is a maze in which the individual can easily become lost. Passivity is the easiest response. Resourcefulness is no longer rewarded.

Quite simply we are losing the ability to resolve our own problems. We have become deskilled in a whole range of areas to which our forebears applied common sense based on experience. From repairing the appliances on which our daily lives now depend to knowing how to respond as parents, from buying good food to rating the success of our love lives, we have become increasingly hesitant and eager for the endorsement of an expert.

Television, newspapers and periodicals deluge us with information and yet that only increases our dependence. To make sense of the conflicting advice, we turn to people who specialize in the subject, hoping that they, at least, should be able to offer a balanced view. Yet the opposite appears to be the case. Who knows what a healthy diet is? How do you make decisions about genetic engineering, test-tube fertilization, euthanasia and abortion? Where are the limits to what is permissible in disciplining children? Who 'owns' the knowledge of how to make life-saving drugs? Who 'owns' information?

As isolated individuals we are losing any basis on which to judge right from wrong and, as a consequence, will be ever more prone to following the herd, becoming swept along in a tide that veers from extreme to extreme, little caring (or even knowing) about the damage that is being done to those who are directly affected when they are caught in the cross-fire of the latest public obsession. In a society dominated by roles, our relationships become increasingly characterized by detachment rather than engagement; a detachment that is reinforced in all aspects of our lives, including our relationship with our environment. Everything is someone else's responsibility.

Being anonymous, answerable to no one, lost in the mass, paying one's taxes, independent of the state are, on the surface, all aspects of a society that values individuality and tolerates difference. All the traditional rights – of speech, association, and so on – appear to be safeguarded but, in reality, offer only a superficial, fickle kind of freedom, one that can be taken away as easily as it is given. Anxiety, depression and a lack of self-esteem lie very close to the surface of our brash, can-do culture. We are chronically unsure of ourselves, even to the extent of knowing who we are. While we may have liberated ourselves from the arbitrary oppression of feudalism and patriarchy, we have put nothing in its place. We are rootless and exposed. Such individuality comes at a price.

The monster of public opinion is an unpredictable beast and few can stand in its path. Martin Neimoeller's summary[11] of the position of the individual in Nazi Germany ('When Hitler attacked the Jews I was not a Jew, therefore I was not concerned. And when Hitler attacked the Catholics, I was not a Catholic, and therefore I was not concerned. And when Hitler attacked the unions and the industrialists, I was not a member of the union and I was not concerned. Then, Hitler attacked me and the Protestant Church – and there was nobody left to be concerned . . .') may seem a long way from contemporary experience, but it conveys the gist of the dangers of living as an isolated individual in a mass society. Sooner or later the spotlight will turn on us, and then who will we turn to for help?

These trends should disturb, not only because of the implications they hold for each of us as individuals, but because prolonged economic difficulties or scarcity of food – exacerbated by the lack of flexibility in the command-and-control decision-making processes – would test our resourcefulness as individuals. We could no longer rely on the social structure to keep delivering the goods.

The collapse of the Russian and Asian economies was mitigated by the continued existence of a black, or barter, economy. Ordinary Russians have always had to live by their wits, and networks of informal trading systems played a significant part in avoiding the shortages that were commonplace throughout the communist era. As the rouble became increasingly worthless, people merely reverted to arrangements that had stood them in good stead in the past. Such relationships barely exist in Western societies and would have to be developed from scratch in the event of a calamity. They need people who are practised and confident in operating outside a command-and-control environment. Where are such individuals to be found?

SUMMARY

The common theme running through this analysis is that there seems to be an 'inner logic' to the way that our society is moving. More than that, we are being pushed in a direction that is both ultimately unsustainable and fundamentally anti-life – the very basis of our civilization is under question. Despite the endless noise and clamour aimed at convincing us that we live in the age of the individual, the opposite is true. All the major engines for change are increasingly global in orientation and geared towards the pursuit of profit. As a consequence, the individual is being marginalized and is effectively expendable when the interests of 'progress' dictate.

Large-scale institutions dominate the social landscape and have an essentially legalistic outlook on the world. Individuals only have significance in so far as they trigger a category that has been defined as being appropriate. Real people are reduced to a few, simple dimensions and their needs are dealt with by a predetermined set of responses that are the same for everyone. In a very real sense, we live in the interstices between these organizational giants, 'free' space that is rapidly dwindling as ever more areas of life are encompassed by rules and regulations.

The problems that this trend inevitably produces in actual lives can only be challenged through the law, either directly to the courts or through appeal to one of the many official and semi-official watchdogs that have become necessary and which themselves are institutional and quasi-legalistic in their approach. Once embroiled in the system, the individual often feels like a bystander and rarely emerges feeling vindicated or even satisfied with the outcome. Kafka-esque is the only way to describe it.

The natural response in these circumstances is passivity (interspersed with outbreaks of mindless violence), a turning of one's back on a world in which one has no personal interest or stake. It is no accident that the structural framework of society is at the macro, institutional level of governments and corporations. What little organization there is at the local level continues to wither from lack of support, prompted by a feeling of 'What's the point?' or 'Why waste energy on something that won't have any impact?'

We have become atoms in an environment that seems to care little whether we live or die. And we, in our turn, are more than ready to pass by on the other side when confronted with need or distress. It is not the soil to nourish individuals who might be able to respond in a crisis or, perhaps equally significantly, might become fired with a new way of looking at life.

Just as all previous civilizations, knowingly or unknowingly, have found themselves imprisoned in a way of life they could not (or did not want to) change and which led inevitably to their decline and collapse, so the trends that are evident in our own day overlap and reinforce one another in a way that does not offer much confidence for the future. We depend on a world economy that is inherently unstable, our agriculture is unsustainable in the longer term, the command-and-control nature of our decision-making processes are unlikely to respond effectively to crisis and, as individuals, we are becoming less and less resourceful and more and more dependent on being serviced.

In a nutshell, people are losing control of their lives. Worse still, it is becoming increasingly difficult to hold on to those virtues that we would see as essentially human. We are like sleepwalkers approaching a precipice: on one level we are aware of the danger, but are compelled against our wills to continue. We need to wake up and set about regaining control of our destinies.

Civilizations fail when their way of looking at the world, and of acting in it, becomes ossified to an extent that people, though many may recognize that things are wrong, are unable to do anything about it. That seems to be the case today. To adapt, we need to be able to step outside the mind-set that currently grips us like a vice and find different, more appropriate ways of thinking and doing.

Ways of the World

If we are to change the way we think and act in the world we must first understand something about the processes that go to shape our ideas about the nature of reality. The images of who we are, the purpose of our existence, even the stuff out of which the environment we inhabit is made, have clearly changed over the centuries. Each age has believed its own view to be the best fit yet and looked disparagingly over its shoulder at what appear to be the quaint or scarcely credible beliefs of earlier times. We are no different, and if we could but see our own assumptions through the eyes of someone living 100 or 500 years in the future we might realize just how tenuous some of our most cherished beliefs really are. That might induce the degree of humility necessary for us to look afresh at the little wood we see around us, appearing so familiar and evidently 'right', and allow us to identify those trees that are worth cultivating, as well as those that are sapping the life-blood from, and threatening the stability of, the whole.

THE LANGUAGE OF LIFE

To illustrate the difficulties we face in thinking about the world, it is helpful to contrast two very different images of the universe we inhabit – both current. In one, we exist as infinitely small atoms in a vast, cold, and ultimately meaningless, collection of gas and other matter, that takes its shape and changes according to the laws of chance; in the other, we are at one with all creation, a living expression of cosmic purpose that provides us with both individual significance and spiritual wholeness. Both views would find strong support and many people would choose elements of each, or select one or the other in a particular context. It is not just a question of heart versus head, of the romantic versus the scientific viewpoint, but of how we come to create such word pictures in the first place. We are able to ask the questions, but coming up with completely satisfactory answers seems to be another matter entirely.

So where do our ideas come from? As I write this paragraph, the words 'appear' in my brain and are translated via my hands on to a computer screen. Once there, I can replace, delete and polish them to my heart's content, but where they originate is a mystery. When my mental processes are on song it feels as if sentences, paragraphs – whole sections – are being summoned from I know not where, taking off in directions that I had not intended; I come up with ideas and images I never knew I had within me. Or so it seems for, clearly, they must come from somewhere within me and the potentialities I embody.

Without wishing to rule out the possibilities of telepathy or some as yet undiscovered ether by which thoughts and ideas can be transmitted, or through which we can 'tune in' to universal truth, it is stretching credibility to accept that such processes play a significant role as I commune with my word processor. More likely is an explanation that has to do with the nature of language and the richness of our social interactions.

Language is a wonderfully flexible and creative mechanism for communication. On an everyday basis we invent combinations of words that are unique and that we, personally, have never uttered before. Twenty words can be rearranged in more ways than there have been seconds since the universe began. Not all those combinations will make sense, but the comparison gives some idea of the potential for originality within even simple sentences. It is the means by which language evolves and meanings change, both for ourselves and society at large.

Ideas, both conscious and unconscious, are constantly being thrown up and tested in the cauldron of daily debate. Some fall on deaf ears, others chime with the times. At any moment, a limited range of themes will be under review, leading to refinements, a deepening of perception and an opening up of fresh lines of enquiry. It is a process in which the ideas we have can hardly be called our own but, in a very real sense, are public property. The fact that I feel moved to comment on the fragility of our civilization is because of a more general interest in these issues. My ideas are a reflection of, and will hopefully resonate with, concerns that are out there as much as within me; in fact, where 'out there' ends and 'me' begins is difficult to determine.

Rather than a universe in which you and I are separate objects interacting on one another like billiard balls endlessly colliding, a more accurate image of the way in which language influences us both is a field of force such as gravity or magnetism. Such fields are difficult to detect; we cannot see gravity, although its effects are obvious enough once we stop to think about them. Force-fields run through us and around us, affecting us in ways that we are hardly conscious of, and they operate at a distance – that is, their influence can extend over large areas so that local events can have often unexpected results elsewhere. Most importantly, you cannot isolate yourself from a field of force in the way that you might in a universe of separate events and objects.

We can begin to see the limitations of a world in which the individual is viewed as a sovereign entity and in which ties and obligations have become eroded to a point where they are all but optional. From such a perspective, the effects of a force-field become increasingly arbitrary and unpredictable. We are tossed around by the winds of change, at the mercy of whatever currents happen to pass us by. There is nothing to anchor us and we are even in danger of losing our sense of self.

Fortunately, the image of a field of force also offers us a hint of how we might regain both purpose and direction, and that is by *strengthening* the links between those closest to us so that, through the way in which we influence language and are influenced by it, we begin to evolve a *shared* view of what is important in life and what we need to do *collectively* to ensure that these priorities are realized in practice. We can regain control of our lives but only through recognizing that we must be part of a set of relationships that represent something larger than ourselves and that, the more meaningful and vital that something is, the more we are likely to experience ourselves as coherent and full of substance. *Community* is the word that comes closest to describing these features, and in gaining a closer understanding of what that concept means we will ultimately find the answers that we are seeking.

This discovering of self through the sharing of self with others is a paradox we will keep returning to but, for the moment, the exploration of language and our responses to it will help us to see how far we can understand life and our part within it. There is an obvious and fundamental difficulty in using language to explain reality. As we experience it, reality is both immediate and continuous. There are no divisions and subdivisions, just a never-ending flow of stimuli. To make sense of it, however, we have to break experience up and fashion it into recognizable shapes and sizes. Language is the main mechanism by which we tie reality down and come to feel that we have gained mastery over it, but it is clearly a fabrication that works more or less well according to the circumstances. Every once in a while, like a cat frozen in car headlights, we encounter something that our carefully crafted edifice has no answer to, and then we are afraid.

Even 'emotion recollected in tranquility' is limited by both Wordsworth's abilities to perceive and the framework of concepts available to him. His poetry may plumb new depths, but it is inevitably selective and an oversimplification compared to reality. Like water sculpting a landscape, language cuts grooves in the smooth, continuous surface of reality – from deep ravines to mere scratches – and our brains accept the familiar contours as if they were the only reality possible.

Like a landscape, however, language evolves and we are hardly aware of the changes. Words are not immutable but change over time, sometimes in subtle, at other times in more dramatic ways. Some words and phrases become worn out through everyday usage, losing any real meaning and acting more as messages of solidarity that demonstrate common membership of a social club ('cool' is an example of a word whose meaning has become so elastic that it is little better than a grunt). One of the strengths of the scientific language is that it appears relatively impervious to such distortion. In theory at least, scientists the world over are likely to draw the same conclusions from the same information.

Science is an example of a specialized language, but it is by no means an isolated one. Most organizations evolve words and phrases that have very specific associations for those involved, but which would either be misinterpreted or misunderstood by outsiders. When the same words can be used in entirely different ways it is not hard to see why negotiations between such structures can be so fraught. The inability to cooperate that characterizes so many institutions that, on the face of it, might seem to have much in common, is one of the more obvious examples – for example, coordinating health initiatives across many departments and agencies. The tendency to reinforce one's position by drafting rules and laws written in one's own language only exacerbates the situation.

Misunderstanding is not restricted to organizations, however: the mutual incomprehension between scientists and non-scientists is a classic example of a clash of cultures. One thought system finds itself apparently challenged by another and the instinctive reactions are attack or defence. Nothing in the opposing view can be allowed to take root, internal purity becomes paramount, and energy is devoted to shoring up one's own position rather than to trying to understand that of the adversary.

The closer our individual philosophies coincide with those of others, the more harmonious our relations are likely to be. Conversely, the nature of language can encourage conflict by exaggerating the differences in people's positions and, in a society such as ours, based on an adversarial system for deciding issues, the need to win can become the sole dynamic, with the consequence that the pursuit of truth becomes an early casualty.

Even within thought systems, battle lines can be quickly drawn up. New scientific theories, for example, usually face fierce opposition from the status quo and the struggle that ensues refines and changes the language of both parties so that, whichever emerges victorious, the world has been changed forever. All language moves on (including the symbolic language of mathematics) and, in that sense, it is doubtful whether Newton, Darwin or Einstein would recognize the theories that are offered up in their names – not because the words or maths have changed but because the meanings ascribed to them have a different resonance.

It is like reading a novel by Jane Austen and believing that we have entered into late 18th-century polite society. What we have done is to enter *our* perception of late 18th-century polite society based on the way we interpret Jane Austen's words in our own day. Experts on a period may be able to determine the facts about an era – for example, that the carpenters of ancient Egypt used the dovetail joint – but they can never know how far their understanding of, and response to, those facts are conditioned by the practices and priorities of their own age. What they must always bear in mind is that those influences will be significant. History may appear to repeat itself, but the lessons of history that a particular age draws are likely to say more about its own preoccupations than the concerns that were important to the people living at the time.

To the ever-changing nature of language and the limited number of issues that a particular culture may consider interesting in a particular era, we may add a third limitation to our understanding of reality, including our place in it and, thus, what our priorities should be. Some experiences are simply more difficult to put into words than others. That may be a reflection of the fact that the matters we wish to explore are not high on the everyday agenda, and we are simply not practised at giving expression to them. In a society that emphasizes the need for objective and repeatable proof, for example, we automatically look for general explanations (even in non-scientific areas such as politics). Many singularities become difficult to describe, particularly if they have made a deep impact on us as individuals. Any account tends to tail off into a semi-apologetic 'I can't really explain it'. In an age of faith, by contrast, the recounting of such experiences would be encouraged and accepted as examples of the wondrous nature of existence. Which is not to say that an age of faith is superior to an age of scepticism, but it is different, and that will be reflected in how easy we find it to express certain experiences.

Another reason why finding the right words can be difficult is that the words themselves do not exist or those that do are such crude approximations that they obscure rather than cast light on an experience. Any culture develops a stock range of everyday language that covers the most common events and issues that are likely to face its users. A society based on agriculture will have a range of words that relate to the seasons, the weather and to the practical tasks of farming that will be totally absent from an urban environment (or, if they do linger on, it will be in the form of stereotypes or approximations that have none of the subtlety of the originals – for example, winter landscapes on Christmas cards bear only a passing resemblance to the reality of winter in the countryside). External reality remains the same; how we view it has changed. The potentiality may continue to exist but is no longer of sufficient importance for us to live it and reflect that living in our language. We would need to reinvent both words and meaning if we were to find ourselves confronting those experiences again.

It is important to look at the nature of language, because it should help us to better come to terms with how we understand the way we experience existence. The discussion thus far suggests that reality is unknowable in the sense that any one of us can encounter, absorb and explain it fully. We experience reality through our senses, mediated by whatever happens within our brain – which is why what our senses 'tell' us can be wrong, because whatever happens is determined, in large measure, by the landscape of the language we inherit and the assumptions it implies about the way things are.

Meaning is created when we put our experience 'into words' (or other symbols, which would include music and art). The words and concepts available at any time are limited and tend to draw a frame around those aspects of reality that we are attuned to recognize. Understanding is thus ultimately allegorical and metaphorical, never absolute. Fairy tales are as valid a way of giving voice to our experience as the first law of thermodynamics (it is just that, in our utilitarian society, the latter has more practical use and our explanations are, therefore, more likely to be couched in scientific terms than in the form of myth).

Language is like a well-beaten track, stretching back into the past as well as into the future. It is in the nature of tracks that they make it easier to move ahead while restricting one's ability to move in other directions. The impact of science on our day-to-day thinking, for example, has tended to push out other, older wisdom into the shadows, from where, just occasionally, it casts a gleam of light that illuminates some experience or event. No sooner has the insight registered, however, than we are being hurried along by our daily round of technologically determined priorities and the moment is lost.

As we have seen, other people are critical to the process of maintaining the sense of being in control. One of the functions of gossip, for instance, is to continually define and redefine the boundaries between what is acceptable and what is not – that is, keeping us on track. On a more fundamental level, however, the role of the 'other' in shaping our perceptions about reality is total. People who, for whatever reason, have been deprived of meaningful human contact develop a distorted sense of their surroundings. The reason is not hard to discover. Without sharing an experience with someone else, it remains only half-formed, half-felt, and we have a sense of something lacking, of something unfulfilled. Until they have been questioned and affirmed (the way in which we gain a sense of being both 'right' and 'all right'), our insights remain untested; they are potential rather than actual. The force-field nature of language suggests that it is only through communication that meaning emerges and truth is finally approached.

One of the pivotal moments in therapy is the bringing of the hidden or unknown into the open and acknowledging it for what it is. The individual is no longer alone and cut off, either from themselves or others. Expression and the acceptance of that expression are, in themselves, healing; bridges have been built and, in the process, the world becomes a different place. Self and other have shared something and both are changed.

The surface minutiae particular to an age (fashion, etiquette, architectural style, and so on) give shape to the landscape and define our day-to-day experience of reality. They provide the background against which we live our lives and appear so self-evident and right that we rarely question their legitimacy. Particularly in a fast-moving society, however, things perceptibly move on and, in that sense, today's truth is tomorrow's falsehood. That does not mean that there is no such thing as absolute truth (science, for example, assumes that reality is ultimately knowable) but that our view of it will always be partial, an approximation that works for a while, but then cracks appear and renovation work is required. Eventually, the papering over becomes obvious to everyone and the hunt is on for an alternative, more appropriate way of looking at the world. It is almost as if we are constantly circling truth, gaining new perspectives but never quite getting into a position where we can see it in its entirety.

Major shifts in perception can be marked by revolution or civil unrest but, more often, they occur without people being aware of how far they have changed. Just as we have an innate ability to learn a language (not specifically English or Swahili, but whatever we are exposed to), so it would appear that we are born with the capacity to absorb a world view. In the same way that it becomes increasingly difficult to learn a new language the older we become, so taking on a new way of looking at the world can be challenging, but not impossible.

Life is a process and we must move with it. The pursuit of truth is about 'becoming', being prepared to face life honestly and openly and being willing to change. It is about questioning reality as it is presented to us through the limitations of the linguistic force-field of which we are a part; it is a two-way process, with the individual both influencing and being influenced by the language they are immersed in.

The passage of a linguistic innovation through a population has been likened to a virus; people become infected and, in turn, pass the germs to others. As an analogy, it has its attractions. We all know how easily influenza can spread, and the sudden appearance of colloquialisms on everybody's lips comes out of the blue, like receiving a dose of something. On a more fundamental level, however, shifts in thinking change us forever, whereas we remain essentially unchanged after a dose of flu. They are also a sign of health rather than disease, and a more helpful comparison is with the maturation process. We all have an innate capacity both to change and to deepen our perceptions about life and, while we might initially accept the dominant thought systems uncritically, experience and reflection change the emphasis; we begin to craft ways of explaining our actions and those of others that is uniquely our own,

51

while still being recognizably part of the mainstream. Occasionally, we may come to realize that what has become important to us is better explained by another way of looking at the world entirely and we, as it were, jump ship. Maturity is knowing ourselves sufficiently well that we can be true to that self in thought and deed.

This uncovering of new layers of meaning is a natural part of being human. Children do it spontaneously and it is a facility that is available to us all throughout our lives, provided we have the courage to face ourselves and the world we inhabit. Although there will always be those who seek to maintain the status quo and those who are eager to seize on the new (it is the struggle between the two that defines the actual tomorrow), hanging on to the past for its own sake is counterproductive. Worse still is the attempt to return to it.

If our ability to perceive the truth is limited by the nature of language in general and compounded by the particular emphases of particular languages at particular times, several conclusions follow:

- We, personally, do not own the language we use. Language exists in the form of a force-field and we are both influenced by that field and have an influence on it. The closer the links we have with other people, the more likely it is that we will evolve a common understanding of issues of mutual interest. By contrast, the looser the links between us, the more likely we are to misunderstand one another.
- We should always distrust language and be seeking to clarify its meaning in any given situation. The more complex the communication and/or the more distance physically, socially or emotionally there is between those involved, the more important this aim becomes.

- We need to recognize that language limits our ability to perceive what is going on around us in so far as it provides well-beaten tracks along which our thoughts can travel effortlessly, distracting us from the truth that lies to either side. We assume that what is must be, rather than seeing it as a reflection of the world we ourselves have created through language. We must always be aware that we may be on the wrong track completely.
- If we seek to be as true to ourselves as we can be, the way that we make decisions is likely to be a more complex process than contemporary experience allows. We have adopted an adversarial approach that demands simple choices between two alternatives – scientist and non-scientist, conservative and radical, employer and employee, innocent and guilty, and so on. The nature of reality outlined above suggests that such concepts and the emphasis on 'right' and 'wrong' are misplaced and may actually contribute to much of the confusion and relativism that pervades our society.
- If our individual views of reality are inevitably partial, it suggests that the more perspectives we can take on board in reaching decisions, the more likely we are to come up with robust solutions to the issues that confront us. That implies being prepared to embrace uncertainty.

It should be clear that one of the problems we face today is that our way of looking at the world ignores all of these safeguards. We talk endlessly at one another and rarely take the time to clarify (television, by its nature, takes it for granted that every viewer approaches its subjects from essentially the same point of view). Our social constructs are inherently conflict-full and necessarily simplistic and we tend to assume that our own point of view is the only one that is relevant to the matter in hand. The track we are currently on runs straight as a die, and the way it is heading is an indication of just how important it is that we find a new direction if we wish to create a more realistic, more sustainable future.

The good news, however, is that just as language constrains and obscures, so it can also liberate and clarify. If only we can find the words and phrases that will throw light into the darkness around us, we can begin to find a new way forward.

Who Do We Think We Are?

With these thoughts in mind, it perhaps becomes easier to see why different ages produce such radically different views of human nature and why, in time, our own assumptions will be overturned and superseded. That does not imply that human nature changes, rather that each age has to confront different issues and therefore 'sees' different aspects of it. Hobbes, for example (writing at the time of the English Civil War), believed that the removal of the restraints of the state, which he suggested was best embodied in monarchy, would lead to 'a war of every man, against every man . . . and the life of man, solitary, poor, nasty, brutish and short'. He saw his methodology as having the rigour of the emerging sciences, underpinned by Descartes' principles of objectivity and reduction. He concluded that fear (of the state) is a necessary precondition for harmonious relations between people.

Two and half centuries later, Freud also believed that his theories were scientific (although he challenged the Cartesian assumption about the pre-eminence of rational thought in human actions) and his work reflects the mechanistic and hydraulic emphases of Newtonian physics. Thus he believed that the benefits and achievements of civilization were the result of psychic energy being channelled from the libido (a much wider instinct than the urge to reproduce – literally, it is the drive to life), allowing peace, order and good government at the expense of anarchic self-fulfilment. Humankind's instincts needed restraining, but the glories of art and science were a compensation for what the individual had been forced to give up through socialization.

Rousseau, by contrast, saw humankind's natural state as being pure and noble, uncorrupted by a civilization that created unnatural desires. The Enlightenment was a time of great hope and confidence in the perfectibility of the human condition and of a virtuous circle between individual self-interest and the common good. Rousseau's collective, general will was the only basis for legitimate sovereignty and was, by definition, in everyone's interest.

Change was in the air, and it was a philosophy that appealed to revolutionaries everywhere. Rousseau was spared the consequences of his vision but, if nothing else, the French Revolution demonstrated that the balance between chaos and order is always a fine one and that the human condition becomes increasingly complex as the number of citizens seeking their share of the good life increases.

One could go on, pointing out the contrasts in the way that the role and nature of women is viewed today and in Victorian times, or in how young men were educated in Sparta compared with the contemporary United States. Each era has a different orientation towards reality determined by a) the physical environment in which people live (we could hardly talk of the brain being hard and soft wired without the existence of computers), b) the different groupings within society and the nature of the social relations between them (we talk of democracy but recognize that class and other forms of social stratification still play an important part in our culture), and c) the major belief systems and the values implicit in them. Language provides the framework that sustains such general features (the 'landscape') and makes them appear inherently reasonable and self-justifying.

There is usually sufficient coherence between these three dimensions for society to muddle along, but it is in the tensions and contradictions that are more or less manifest that the potential for change exists. It is again through language and the way it develops that these discrepancies are revealed and resolved. Because individuals take language for granted – that is, they do not invent it, they are absorbed into it – and because it is so all-embracing, the way that such fault-lines reveal themselves will reflect, by definition, the world view they emerge from and point in certain directions rather than others. As far as culture is concerned, there is no such thing as a blank sheet; no one has ever invented an entirely new philosophy that marked a complete break with the past. Rather, a different way of looking at life is suggested by, and grows out of, what already exists, by freshening up bits here, recycling bits there. It develops organically rather than springing fully formed on to the world stage.

To continue the metaphor of culture as a track that takes people in certain directions rather than others, the three dimensions tend to run in parallel and thereby reinforce one another. The more the three are synchronized, the harder it becomes both to envisage an alternative and to exert the leverage that is necessary to overcome the momentum that is carrying the edifice ever onwards. Only when one strand begins to diverge from the rest or its contribution weakens for some reason, is there is a real opportunity for a significant change in direction.

Once in train, divergence can tend towards the exponential, with each step suggesting the next until a new equilibrium is reached and a new bearing confirmed. Like a spacecraft leaving the earth, however, there is a critical point before which there is always the danger of the draw of the old dragging the initiative back into the familiar grooves of thought and consigning it to the dustbin of interesting ideas that might have been. That is why thought without deeds, the practical ways in which we breathe life into our thinking and thereby actually change the world, never gets off the ground.

DOING IT OUR WAY

What, then, are the themes that define our particular ways of looking at the world and how coherent are they? More than anything else we remain the inheritors of the Enlightenment, with its emphasis on empiricism, naturalism and materialism, and it is likely that any large-scale changes in the way we think and act will come from a reassessment of the key themes and concepts that have come to form part of our everyday thinking.

The liberal viewpoint emphasizes the centrality of the individual. Our current interpretation of that legacy is fashioned firstly by what might be called the 'human development movement', a broadly based church that embraces insights from the neo-Freudians to person-centred counselling and takes in the more frankly commercial schools of self-help and self-development along the way. Although authorities such as Carl Rogers always emphasized the importance of the 'other' in the development of 'self', the tendency has been to focus on the individual and how they might improve the quality of their lives. Self-fulfilment has become the name of the game and it is everyone's right to enjoy a piece of the action. From this point of view, life is seen as a process and it is not unusual to hear people saying that we are all born with the potential to 'become' someone. It is a commonplace observation to say that Shakespeare, Newton, Mother Theresa and each one of us shared broadly similar experiences as we grew to adulthood.

We explain how we develop by reference to a number of distinct but overlapping dimensions. It is now generally accepted that our genetic inheritance determines our basic natures – even down to what sort of disease is likely to kill us. The study of genetics seems destined to show that our behavioural patterns are predetermined at birth (depression, criminality and promiscuity are all said to have a genetic basis, although the linkage between the two is unlikely to be so simplistic), but there is also an acceptance that the environment in which we live is crucial in determining how we grow and develop.

For all the reasons suggested by our brief look at language, the culture into which we are born will be a clear determinant of both the experiences we are likely to have and the options that will be available to us: a child born into an affluent Western family will face very different challenges and opportunities from someone born in a shantytown in South America. This context might also encourage or discourage any innate tendencies to depression, criminality and promiscuity, etc.

We also accept that, in growing to adulthood, a child passes through developmental stages and that, at each stage, there are tasks or challenges that require a successful response (or adaptation) if we are to mature successfully; these include the ability to trust,[1] to become autonomous, to achieve identity, intimacy, and so on. If something goes wrong at any stage – and this may be due to general patterns of child rearing (including the impact of peer group pressure at school, for example) or to single, traumatic events – there may be consequences in later life. The direction of the process – its purpose, if you like – is integration, a 'ripening', to paraphrase Erikson's words,[2] 'of the fruit of these stages' in which the individual finds peace through gaining a sense of meaning about their individual existence. Hence the popular concept of life as a journey with a goal in view (which is hardly a new idea, as suggested by the myth of the Holy Grail).

The pursuit of self-realization is an essentially optimistic view of human nature, reflecting the stable nature of Western society since the end of the Second World War, the existence of welfare systems that, in theory at least, provide for everyone's basic need for food and shelter, and an emphasis on merit rather than position (anyone can achieve their dreams if they have the talent and drive). If the circumstances are right we will be all right, and a growing army of therapists and counsellors are available to help us over obstacles and blockages that may be current, or the legacy of past traumas and bad experiences. Evil is, by definition, the result of unhappy circumstances and can always be ameliorated with sufficient energy and resources. The future *can* be better than the past.

This view of what it means to be human is so pervasive that it is hardly challenged. The individual rules – end of story. The earlier comments about the force-field nature of language and its impact on the concept of individuality suggest that, at the very least, there may be a need to reappraise the place of the individual in the scheme of things. Our associational concepts, which root the individual in a network of relationships and mutual obligations, appear to be falling apart in front of our eyes. Family, marriage, neighbourliness and community are fast becoming as obsolete and as lacking in meaning as the seasons are in our everyday lives. The world we inhabit becomes ever more akin to the cold, 'atomic' universe governed by chance, and increasingly estranged from any sense of being at one with creation and the rest of humankind.

We do not know what that future holds, but of one thing we can be certain: future generations will view human nature quite differently. That fact alone should give us pause for thought.

COMING TO TERMS WITH OUR UNCONSCIOUS

Our current view of how we come to be the individuals we are thus has several strands: firstly, our genes; secondly, how we cope with the challenges of growing up; and, thirdly, the particular culture into which we are born and our place in it. It is a profoundly complex interweaving of cause and effect that is difficult to unravel at an individual, let alone a species, level. When you add our limited understanding of the unconscious, with its potential to dissemble, justify itself and generally conceal and confuse our basic motivations from everyone including ourselves, it becomes easier to see why we should approach the issue of trying to understand the human condition with extreme caution.

Fate is an old-fashioned word. From our standpoint as sophisticated materialists, we are more likely to explain a person's pattern of choosing unsuitable partners as being the result of an abusive childhood; or to see a death from cancer as a genetic predisposition to contract the disease. That does not stop us from repeating past mistakes ourselves or help us to change lifestyles that are obviously unhealthy. We know very little about the processes that determine what happens to us. Nevertheless, to suggest that we are driven by forces we do not understand is unscientific.

To Freud (who 'discovered' and named the unconscious), life was a constant battle between Eros and Thanatos – the drive towards life and towards death. It is important to recognize that both are inherent in our natures and that, although Thanatos always triumphs in the end, life is only bearable when Eros is successfully keeping its darker companion at bay. From that tension comes not only the ways we feel and act in practice but, in the eternal clash between order and chaos (from dealing with delinquency to keeping the house clean), the wider challenges that face both us and society. How we respond can be healthy and life-affirming or obsessive and maladaptive. In one we are in control of our destinies, in the other we become the victims of our fate.

The problem is that it is sometimes difficult to know where the balance lies in our own lives. We may believe that we have life taped, but it is often in precisely those circumstances that we are heading for a fall. To be sure of oneself can be hubris in disguise and it is a feature of our society that it feels both supremely confident and out of the control of any of us. Humour is often a way of exploring fears that cannot be voiced more openly and there is a joke about our increasing dependence on computers that runs, 'The last time we entrusted ourselves so completely to technology it hit an iceberg and sank!'

However much we may try to create certainty, the common factor we all share is that we don't know where fate is taking us. It may be leading us to play an unknowing part in someone else's tragedy. It may be that we are on some latter-day *Titanic*, believing that we live in the best of all possible worlds. It may be that there is a brighter, better world just around the corner. Wherever we are headed, our capacity to exercise some control over our future depends on our ability to understand our actions and where they may be leading. Free will is only meaningful when we understand why we feel pushed in one direction rather than another. Only then do we have the opportunity to override the impulse and make a 'free' decision. Without such awareness we are continually being driven by forces that may, or may not, be in our best interests; our lives have become determined – we are fated.

Freud believed that only through understanding the forces of our unconscious do we stand a chance of overcoming or reversing our fate. To act without knowing what we are doing or why, is one certain route to destruction. The Temple of Apollo at Delphi carried the inscription 'Know Thyself' carved into its stonework. In the myth that carries his name, Oedipus thought he knew exactly who he was and thereby unwittingly set in train the events that led him to murder his father and marry his mother. Self-knowledge makes us all more secure. Fate only becomes evident in retrospect. In that sense we are always potentially in the first act of a tragedy of our own making. Each decision we make is potentially fate-full.

Seen from this perspective, it becomes easy to understand the way in which individuals, groups and nations almost fall into conflict. The less aware we are of ourselves and our environment, the more we depend on assumptions. As we have seen, those assumptions depend on self-contained thought systems that lead us, often erroneously, to believe that we understand what others are doing and saying. When we are unsure of their intentions, those assumptions are more likely to be negative; what we see is a threat, a put down, or an attempt to take advantage. We are also more likely to 'project' our own inadequacies, blind spots and fears on to others and become angry with them for displaying traits that are really our own. Once we have made an assumption we will see the evidence to support it because we expect to see it, and every act will be interpreted from that viewpoint. A vicious circle has been set in train that, if it is not interrupted, will inevitably lead to collision.

Feuds are a classic example of how the complex dynamics between individuals and groups can take on a life of their own, passing from generation to generation as if it were the most natural thing in the world. At their root, however, such disputes are invariably the result of faulty assumptions about others that have resulted in rigid interpretations of events and a focus of emotion that can find no other outlet. At some level we all need scapegoats. Only increasing self-awareness can keep this destructive side of our natures in check.

Although domestic violence is commonplace, its sporadic nature shows that it is easier to reverse these tendencies at the interpersonal level – where face-to-face contact brings people back to reality – than with larger groupings. When a nation, for example, begins to feel aggrieved with a neighbour (usually because of its own shortcomings) everything gets blamed on them and it becomes increasingly difficult to stem the all-consuming and outright hostility that emerges with frightening speed and ferocity. A kind of madness takes over and has to run its course before reason and compassion can reassert themselves. We have only just begun to come to terms with dealing with humanity on a global scale, and even a casual glance at our own history suggests that our ability to handle disputes on this scale is extremely limited. Trying to increase our awareness in an effort to prevent such an inevitable escalation has to be a more creative and life-affirming response than picking up the pieces afterwards.

There is another way in which trying to access our unconscious is important. For Jung (in contrast to Freud, who saw it as a realm of unresolved conflicts and neuroses), the unconscious was the font of human creativity and spirituality. The 'collective unconscious' exists at an even deeper level than the personal unconscious and is a repository of a deep wisdom acquired over the generations of human existence. It becomes manifest in art and dreams and is represented symbolically in archetypal terms. Jung believed that the 'archetypes' pre-exist us as individuals; in other words, like our instincts, they are inherited and a basic part of our psyche (although the archetypes themselves are unchanging, Jung believed that how they come to consciousness will vary from individual to individual and culture to culture).

Accessing the archetypes can provide insights that are difficult to put into words, and thus stand in stark contrast with our need to be specific, to have certainty in our lives. Frequently ambiguous, they fly in the face of our craving to be able to say we are for something or against it. There is the hint that, once again, reality is more complex than we are willing, or perhaps yet able, to accept. Developing skills in understanding the manifestations of the archetypes, and thereby tapping into not only the essence of our humanity, but also that which links us to the wider realm of nature, is a project that we need to undertake as never before if we are to reverse our increasing detachment from the world around us.

We need to develop ways of engaging with one another that will not only minimize the opportunities for misunderstanding, but will do so by celebrating and utilizing difference in the endless and creative pursuit of fresh meaning.

Only in that way will we continue to develop as human beings and avoid a zombie-like existence of certainty, confined in a linguistic straitjacket and in constant fear of apparently anarchic and dangerous forces 'out there'.

ENTER THE SCIENTIFIC VIEWPOINT

If ultimately we can never know reality, and what we believe we know is likely to be distorted by the workings of our unconscious, then the scientific viewpoint, which is sceptical, systematic, and spurning of superstition and faith, should be an ally in helping us to take an honest look at ourselves and our place in the universe. However, science has come to play such a commanding role in how we view the world that effectively it underpins our generally individualistic and materialist culture. And therein lies its problem. It is not neutral, but deeply embedded and implicated in the culture that has brought it into being. There is a symbiotic relationship in which each is dependent on the other. Our day-to-day language not only reflects its dominant position, but also reinforces its apparent infallibility as an explanation of reality. It now defines the track that we appear forced to follow and bundles us along at a pace that is unprecedented in human history. We no longer have even the time to stop and take our bearings.

As an example of the Janus-headed nature of the scientific method, of its ability to throw light into corners that have never been visible before while, at the same time, casting human affairs into yet deeper darkness, a look at the impact of our growing understanding of genetics is illuminating. There is now a general acceptance of evolution both as a theory and as a paradigm for everyday experience; we talk of everything – from cars to social groupings – evolving. The idea that, along with the rest of the natural world, we have evolved from common ancestors has had a dramatic impact on how humankind views itself. In many ways we are still reeling from the implications of having to acknowledge that we are simply animals and not singled out in any way. We may have always accepted our base – that is, animal – instincts, but we preferred to relegate them to the back room, reserving our culture and knowledge for public viewing; Darwin and Freud have stripped us bare of any such pretence.

Nevertheless, a reintegration of humankind into the natural world should help us to recognize that we need to find our proper niche in the scheme of things rather than always assuming that the scheme of things will fit in with us. It should help us to establish a sense of direction that is compatible with the health of the environment that we share with the rest of creation. A change in direction does not necessarily imply movement that is newer, faster, bigger or better – all fundamental aspects of progress as currently defined; it might suggest going deeper, seeking, for example, a greater awareness of ourselves and our potential. Common sense suggests that such an orientation is likely to require us to be more in touch with the natural world and the processes that support both us and it.

On the face of it, the study of genetics – the powerhouse driving evolution – is about gaining a greater understanding of what makes us tick as human beings, how we have come to be the way we are and what distinguishes us from other species. It should provide a basis from which we can both improve the human condition and begin to explore what concepts such as 'self-realization' and 'self-development' might mean.

That is not happening – quite the reverse. The reality is that the science of genetics has reached a point where it has nothing to do with people at all and everything to do with a corporate world that is, at the end of the day, about continuing growth and profitability. Big business has become the major force behind the production of genetically modified foods (through agribusiness) and the eradication/prevention of disease by drug companies fighting for their share of hard-pressed welfare programmes (centrally administered bureaucracies that have lost sight of what it means to be healthy). Private organizations are interested in the cloning of humans and animals, eager to exploit the distress caused by infertility or the loss of a beloved pet.

The boundaries between pure research and its application have become so blurred that the latter effectively dictates the agenda of the former. Budgets, even in universities, are funded by industry and very few scientists working in the field can be said to be truly independent. Research is conducted behind closed doors and knowledge is jealously guarded. Media-focused events (complete with photo-opportunities), such as the cloning of Dolly the sheep, become as important as understanding either the science or the implications of such 'breakthroughs'.

The study of genetics has an immense investment in the status quo. It is part of the alliance of forces that are pushing us ever further down the cultural track that is threatening our civilization. Far from providing the ideas and language that might change the way we look at life, its voice is among the most strident elements in the daily call to believe that only through progress will the troubles of the world be resolved. It now depends on that assumption for its credibility.

Progress as we currently understand it is schizophrenic. Genetics may still offer the promise of new technologies to take the pain out of daily living but, for an example of what happens when a scientific breakthrough is taken over and exploited by the institutional world, one has only to look at the nuclear industry. Quantum mechanics was once the wonder of the age. It was new and seemed to offer infinite possibilities. Pundits talked about free power for all and of miracles in health care just around the corner. Particularly during the Second World War and immediately afterwards, money and resources were poured into developing its applications.

The results have hardly justified the claims that were once made. Certainly, there have been benefits – radiology, for example – but, in the main, the results have been to increase the very problems that make life appear beyond the control of individuals – large, impersonal corporations bent on self-justification and self-defence, regulated by equally large watchdogs that have vague powers and appear largely unaccountable. The impact has lodged deep; the threat of nuclear war/terrorism has haunted our psyches for half a century and the safety record of nuclear power stations means that they may be out of sight but, after Chernobyl, they are never out of mind. The same kind of fears are surfacing about the potential uses of genetics. For every advance a raft of new problems is created – that's progress.

The promise of higher yield, more pest-resistant crops may sound like a wonderful opportunity to rid the world of hunger – food being the basic requirement for anyone's self-development – until you realize that the cost (especially in poor countries) is the scenario painted in the previous chapter – of once self-sufficient farmers being thrown into urban poverty because they cannot afford the repayments on the loans they have taken out to buy the new crop varieties. As Sarah Sexton has pointed out,[3] people starve not because there is insufficient food (the UN World Food Programme, for example, estimates that there are one and half times the amount required currently available), but because they do not have access to land to grow food to feed themselves or cannot earn the cash to buy the food they need from markets. Poverty and lack of empowerment, not shortage of food, is the root cause of hunger, and genetically modified crops – like the much heralded 'green revolution' before them – will actually fuel poverty by bankrupting farmers and thereby adding to the ever growing problem of the rootless urban poor.

We are so used to the idea that science represents progress – the quest for new knowledge, new opportunities – that it is difficult to accept the idea that it now represents something of a dead end. The reason is not so much science – which provides, and will continue to provide, a valid way of looking at the world – but the fact that the only way in which it can operate effectively in the modern world is through its alliance with the institutional world. Just as money becomes destructive when it is driven by a global obsession with speculation, so science only began to come off the rails when it became bankrolled by big business in its pursuit of profit. In fact, science and industry are now so entwined that it is difficult to see how they might ever separate again.

It is in this climate that it becomes easier to understand how scientists can be working flat out and competing with one another to isolate 'terminator' genes (or induce sterility in other ways) that will cause any seeds saved for planting to die before they germinate, thus forcing farmers to buy new seed each year from the producer – very profitable if it can be achieved, but having little to do with expanding our horizons, alleviating hunger or growing better crops. The fact that a corporation in New York or London shows increasing profits, while a country in Africa is forced to cut welfare programmes to its urban poor to service the debts that create those profits, is not an issue. The institutional world is intrinsically amoral and anti-life because it forgot about people long ago. Science has become its willing accomplice.

So Which Way Are We Headed?

The dominant mind-sets in our culture are clearly operating at different levels and effectively in opposition to one another. A commitment to the individual defines our social relationships, while the pursuit of economic growth, driven by the alliance between science and the corporate world, is our clearest statement of belief. In the first case, language is elliptical, descriptive and often unique to the individual using it (all the elements, in fact, that go to create the diversity that is individuality). In the second, it is detached, concrete, numerate, ordered, consistent and accessible to people across the globe (the characteristics of the institutional world).

It is no accident that these characteristics reflect the polarity that is inherent between the feminine and masculine principles, nor that the increasing imbalance between them mirrors the dominance of the latter over the former in our everyday life. Polarization is a symptom of disease, and common sense suggests that it is in the middle ground, between the untrammelled pursuit of individuality on the one hand and the institutional juggernaut on the other, that the way forward is to be found.

It is important to emphasize that the masculine and feminine principles are only indirectly related to gender in the sense that women are more likely to manifest the feminine side and men the masculine. In practice, the majority of flesh and blood people occupy a narrow section within the wider continuum that exists between the two poles; their actual behaviour will also vary according to the context of the moment. Thus, although increasing numbers of women are breaking into positions of corporate influence and power, the trend towards 'masculinity' continues. The culture of the institutional world is inescapably masculine and women have to employ that side of their natures to succeed, thus perpetuating the dangerous detachment that is destroying our social fabric. By recognizing these pressures – by knowing ourselves better – we can begin to look for alternative ways of acting in the world that might encourage a more balanced application of the masculine and feminine principles.

As suggested earlier, it is precisely when major discrepancies arise in the patterns of thinking in a culture that real change becomes a possibility. Not only is it easier to switch to parallel tracks, but the chance of being able to set off in entirely different directions is increased. The fact that a person-centred belief in the individual can exist alongside an institutional juggernaut that cares nothing for human life is therefore a real opportunity, but only when we recognize that the latter is winning hands down and that we urgently need to do something to reverse the polarity.

If we are genuinely seeking to put people first, we need to review the relationship between them and wider society to ensure that there is both the capacity and the commitment to nurture and encourage true individuality. A starting point is to recognize that the way of looking at the world that has brought us to where we are today is no longer the liberating force that it once was. A thought system that has brought ever increasing wealth, knowledge and mastery over nature at the institutional level has also produced greater loneliness, anxiety and fear in the everyday lives of people.

As individuals, scientists may understand that their endeavour is part of the patient building of a model, but the collective impact is to present a framework that is widely regarded as the truth. The very language of science has become so central to our thinking precisely because it appears to explain and justify so much of our daily experience, from switching on the electric light to listening to news of some technological marvel on our televisions – in other words, a daily experience it has created and fashioned. Like the medieval church, it has become a self-explaining and, therefore, a self-fulfilling prophecy. If we are to open up a new track, we will have to discover a new wisdom (or, like an urban dweller settling on the land, rediscover and build on an old one). Only by breathing new life into words and phrases that might serve this purpose can we hope to fashion a different and more hopeful future.

Science and materialism are now on the side of the status quo. They are part of the problem and leading us ever further away from an emphasis on the individual that was once its greatest achievement. We need to rid ourselves of three key assumptions. Firstly, that there is always a 'right' answer to every problem: science has rooted the adversarial approach firmly in everyday life with its emphasis on a hypothesis being either 'right' or 'wrong' (the reality of personal existence is that two apparently incompatible solutions can both be 'right' and that progress lies in resolving that apparent paradox). Secondly, that with sufficient resources and intelligence, all of life's problems can be solved (an approach that leads, for example, to the belief that, if only enough money was put into the health service, it would become efficient and effective, obscuring the reality that a centrally run bureaucracy may have little impact on how healthy or unhealthy we become, no matter how much cash is injected into the system). Finally, that only those aspects of the truth that are accessible to the scientific method are worth pursuing (hence the inability of mainstream science to engage with alternative medicine). We need to recognize the kind of rut that we are in before we can begin to climb out of it.

If You Believe That, You'll Believe Anything

At another level altogether, the study of evolution demonstrates a fundamental human need: our need to believe in something outside and greater than ourselves. Traditionally, religion has fulfilled this function, but the advance of science in general, and of evolutionary theory in particular, has made religious dogma harder to accept. In fact, many commentators on genetics and evolution see no need to assume any process beyond that of evolution itself. Explanations exist that show how primitive organisms first came into being and a direct line can be drawn to ourselves with the aid of genes, the processes of genetic mutation and the general operation of evolution.

The idea of humankind having any purpose other than as the transmitter of a hugely successful gene complex is therefore entirely redundant. We may wonder at the beauty of nature, be proud of our achievements as a civilization, and be driven to yet greater discoveries and understanding, but these are all an accidental by-product of a process that is its own justification. It started fortuitously, has lurched from one crisis to another and will continue to wander aimlessly according to its own internal logic. In evolutionary terms, we are a sideshow, an interesting one but one that was neither destined to happen nor has any special significance in the scheme of things.

But that view is only a belief, a way of looking at the world that makes sense to the believer. As geneticist David

Suzuki has pointed out,[4] students of genetics today laugh at what scientists understood as little as 30 years ago, while accepting that what they are being taught is the absolute truth. There is increasing evidence that the deterministic model of genetics currently dominant is simply wrong and that, once again, reality is far more complex. That does not diminish the belief of orthodoxy's adherents. Science may be built on scepticism but, as human beings, we need to believe in something. It is what gives us our sense of significance which, as evolutionists would probably point out, we need if we are to survive.

This craving for certainty seems to be part of our nature, but we must be aware of its limitations. It becomes positively dangerous when it is based on oversimplifications and standardized responses to life's problems because it leads to a complacency that can produce a violent and intolerant reaction when challenged (one of the fundamental charges against religious dogma has always been that it reduces something mystical and obscure to a set of fixed formulae whose content is even further diluted by endless repetition).

In that sense, the belief that genes explain everything is akin to the 'God is in his heaven, all's right with the world' kind of comfort that it seeks to replace. Equally, the idea that we are nothing but our genes and that, one day, they may be used to predict our futures, is really astrology in another form, reflecting our need to know that life has some form or meaning. Believing that certain things are preordained lightens the burden of individual responsibility. It is a retreat from the challenge of being alive.

The Paradoxical View of Life

Like all other ways of looking at the world, evolution represents both a partial truth and one that is deeply embedded in the culture that espouses it. The one thing that we can be sure about is that in 200 years' time people will have very different handles on which to hang their thinking about reality. Rather than pretend that language is precise and that what we believe is the truth, we ought to make a virtue of necessity and accept the uncertainty of being as a strength.

It makes sense to see the various thought systems we possess as tools that are more or less useful in the particular circumstances we face and to use them accordingly. Looking from several perspectives at the problems we face, both as individuals and as a society, can offer insights that lead to a one-off amalgam that fits the issues better than any of the perceptions on their own. By juxtaposing very different views of what is apparently 'out there', we might just find that, momentarily, a problem moves into clearer focus.

The task, therefore, is not to construct another all-embracing cathedral of thought in which people can believe absolutely, but to orientate ourselves in a way that allows the natural creativity of language to look at a problem from every angle, before suggesting a frame of reference that will be uniquely applicable to it. The 'atomic' view of nature may be relevant in some circumstances, the 'holistic' in others, a combination in yet others. Rather than one mind-set needing to conquer all others, the emphasis will be on open-minded questioning.

At the heart of this way of thinking lies the paradox. Our scientific frame of reference leads us time and again to attempt to reduce problems to simple one-liners: 'x' is the result of 'y' or 'z'. Thus, an increase in delinquency is caused by declining family values, poverty, cuts in police budgets, materialism, opportunities for mobility, or whatever axe you are keen to grind at the particular moment. Policies are framed on this basis and scarce resources directed accordingly. Sometimes there is an 'improvement' in the situation, but usually there is a need to address some more pressing crisis and we forget about or learn to live with the original problem.

The truth is that reality is far too complex and contradictory to be reduced to a statement of cause and effect. At the heart of almost every issue that we are prepared to face openly and honestly lies a paradox, a set of conclusions or statements that are contradictory. The idea of the individual is an example. It has already been suggested that, to be truly individual, we need other people. To recognize that we cannot discover ourselves without engaging in ever closer relations with others is inherently paradoxical.

In certain circumstances, it will be appropriate to emphasize our needs as an individual, in others the importance of our group as a whole or particular members in it. No simple rule can be derived that will be effective in all circumstances. Each situation requires its own analysis without preconceptions. This kind of thinking asks us to try to look at things from several points of view and either to integrate the different perspectives into some new whole that is appropriate for the issue at hand, or to decide which has priority in the present circumstances alone.

In looking for ways forward, ends are always be more important than means, and the way in which the institutional world has lost sight of what it means to be human should be a reminder of the constant need to clarify the values that we would want to underpin the solution to any problem. Is what we are doing taking us closer to where we want to be or further away? Values, visions and beliefs are matters of faith. They represent flags to rally around in the chaotic swirl of everyday life; here I take my stand.

All too often, however, they remain half-formed, unexpressed and unexamined, and, for that very reason, end up being defended simply because they appear to be under attack. The more we can put what we believe to be important in life into a coherent framework, the more these values will work for us and the more we will discover the similarities with others' points of view rather than the differences. They will also provide a reference point in dealing with paradox.

What we must learn to believe in is life itself (including, but not exclusively, human life), its essential 'rightness' and wisdom. We are, after all, part of it; we have also evolved in a way that ensures that the fit is absolute and seamless, like a glove to a hand. Such an approach implies experiencing the world as openly as we can. It will engage our whole self – the rational and the intuitive – but one test of its authenticity will lie in our ability to express our experience clearly through the medium of symbols (which would include poetry, painting and music as well as language). The exploration of meaning will be its hallmark, while recognizing that the ceaseless search for 'truth' should never become dependent on, or tied down by, thought-systems. We will need a stock of concepts that encourage that opening up of perception rather than tying it down by limiting the way we think. Assumptions should always be challenged and, acknowledging the complexity of life, will produce a belief in our ability to find a way forward that fulfils both our potential (destiny even) as a species and recognizes our place in the natural world and our dependence upon it.

BACK TO BASICS

Paradoxically, evolutionary theory has much of value to offer about the nature of existence. At a time when the life that our children will lead seems to be preordained at birth and determined by one institutional force or another, the suggestion that we have evolved over aeons of time should make us question whether the social reality in which we currently live is adapted to us, or whether we have adapted to it. And, if the latter, how far from our evolved selves are we being asked to travel and what is the cost to our individual psyches of being wrenched out of ways of relating to each other and the world at large that are deeply embedded within us?

We believe that evolution is an infinitely slow process, but a brief look at how the life experiences of ordinary human beings have altered in only 100 years shows that we have faced dramatic changes in an evolutionary blink of an eyelid. Unlike any other animal, our view of the world, superficially at least, is capable of rapid and considerable change. Our natures may be plastic but they are not infinitely so, and understanding our evolutionary legacy may help us to discover the limits beyond which it becomes unhealthy to stray. Social evolution may be driven by laws that are markedly different from those that propel physical, or even mental, evolution, but there is a relationship between them that must be respected if we, as organisms, are to survive, let alone thrive.

In her book *The Continuum Concept*,[5] for example, Jean Liedloff contrasted childhood experiences in the Western world with those of the Yequana, a tribe living in the upper Caura river basin, close to the Brazilian border. Her thesis is that the 'continuum' of evolution – that slow, steady aggregation of positive adaptation – creates expectations in the child as to the kind of world it will inhabit. Just as its eyes and ears are tuned to the experiences they are likely to encounter (dogs come into the world with a different set of expectations and their capacities for hearing and smell are correspondingly different), so the infant's emotional and physical development from total dependence to self-reliance is mapped out (it has, for example, innate tendencies to suckle, crawl and explore, and a range of emotional responses to accompany them). These ancestral expectations are then overlaid by its actual experience, and the greater the disparity between the two, the less the individual's inherent potential for wellbeing will be supported.

Childhood with the Yequana is inseparable from everyday living. For the first six months the child never leaves its mother's side while she goes about her normal daily routines; in fact, Liedloff suggests that nothing in the expectations that evolution has laid down can prepare an infant to be left alone or to receive no response when it cries. This extension of the physical and psychic bond in the womb provides a stable base from which the child can begin to develop self-reliance. From that point, the child is allowed to find its own way (a concept of education that is a far cry from our increasingly institutional education system with its national curriculum and emphasis on knowledge that has little day-to-day applicability). The growing child comes to rely on its own in-built sense of danger and increasing involvement in the daily activities of the tribe (appropriate to its developing skills) to find its own unique contribution as an adult. Although life was rigidly divided along gender lines, two aspects of Yequanan life particularly struck Liedloff: the absence of significant unhappiness and an approach to spending time that made no distinction between work and non-work.

It is easy to over-romanticize 'simple' societies, but Liedloff's message to the Western world was straightforward: when mothers realized that 6 months of carrying their baby around would lead to 15 to 20 years of trouble-free child-rearing thereafter, they would adapt their approach. Experience seemed to bear her out. Mothers who had read her book reported that the more they held their babies, the more they wanted to.

Unfortunately, the pressures on mothers to see themselves as something more than staying at home (because, in our culture, work and home are completely different worlds, and work is child-free), combined with pressures from the workplace to return and the need to earn a living, mean that children are effectively separated both from their mothers at birth and from mainstream life until they become adults. Put very simply, we no longer honour motherhood (the very essence and visible expression of the life-force) and place it at the centre of all we do; rather, we expect mothers to fit the rearing of children into a system of structuring reality that is essentially anti-life.

Women find it easier to go with the flow. As Liedloff herself puts it, one of our deepest impulses is to do what is expected of us. The conclusion being suggested is not that a mother holding her baby for the first six months of its life is the solution to all society's ills (which is simplistic thinking), but rather that we need to re-create multi-dimensional patterns of child-rearing that place the child at the centre of the community's life, where evolution clearly expects it to be.

A second cluster of insights that evolution offers is around the nature and extent of our relationships. Put very simply, humankind evolved in a way that puts a premium on co-operation in relatively small groupings. In our vast anonymous cities where several million people can congregate and, to a greater or lesser extent, be dependent on one another, it is easy to forget that, for most of our history, survival depended on effective communication between bands of individuals who knew one another intimately. Maintaining a supply of food, providing shelter and security, and successfully rearing the next generation (in other words, meeting people's basic needs) became essentially social activities and our increasing skills as social animals evolved in this context.

We are group animals and much of the dynamics between individuals in a group is on autopilot, with subtle shifts in body language and other non-verbal cues. Many studies have shown how overwhelming the urge to conform to what are perceived to be group norms can be, even to the extent of denying the evidence of our own eyes.[6] For most of the time we are not even aware of how our behaviour is shaped by those around us and it is that lack of self awareness that has so often proved disastrous.

The residue of these formative experiences is not hard to find. Research has shown[7] that an effective discussion, with everyone participating on an equal basis, becomes virtually impossible if numbers rise above four. Twelve seems to be a natural limit in terms of maintaining intimate connections over a period of time (the size of juries and sports teams) and 150 the limit to the number of people we can relate to effectively – in other words, knowing and understanding enough about them and their relationships, both with ourselves and others in the group, for them to stand out from the crowd. Beyond that, although there may be other orders of magnitude in common usage (neighbourhoods, parishes, political constituencies, and so on), we rapidly lose the human content of any relationships that may exist. It becomes increasingly easy for us to see others as objects and as threats, with all the attendant dangers that have been discussed already.

It should not be assumed that, just because we can only relate to relatively small groupings, large conurbations are necessarily a bad thing. We are aware of how limiting, claustrophobic and intolerant tightly knit communities can be. The individual is often forced to sacrifice their individuality to be accepted and such groupings are inherently conservative and unlikely to be able to respond to major challenges. And, for better or worse, almost unimaginable numbers of human beings are alive and cities provide the only way yet developed of meeting their needs.

The health of those people, however, depends on their having access to the kinds of networks outlined, and that is why 'work' is such an obvious magnet (and why women feel cut off 'at home') when it brings people into contact with one another and provides some kind of purpose for their association. Cities as containers for people may continue, but the way their citizens relate to one another must evolve along radically different lines in the future and be far, far richer in the opportunities that are offered for group activity.

It is worrying to note that, while society becomes generally more and more organized, the kinds of nodes around which community groupings might cohere are continuing to atrophy. At that level, loneliness, insecurity, alienation and aggression are all increasing. With government and business increasingly being national or global in orientation and pursuing their own priorities (which are not about people as individuals), our innate desire for meaningful relationships suggests that there is an urgent need to re-establish them at a local level. For such a development to occur there would have to be a corresponding transfer of real power so that people had something to cooperate about.

The Uncertainty Principle

The emergence of ecology (which is an interesting example of a science-based, but not (yet) institutionally determined, philosophy) is offering us a radically different set of images to contrast with the hi-tech marvels of corporate evolution. Ideas such as 'strength in diversity', the 'need for balance' and the 'interconnectedness of all living organisms' are entering mainstream language. We think increasingly in terms of systems and organic metaphors rather than mechanical ones.

Such word pictures offer the potential for a more integrated, holistic view of life but, for all the reasons discussed (the difficulties inherent in language, the partiality of belief systems, etc), it will be one that is less certain, that shifts as circumstances change, and recognizes that moving purposefully in one direction may have unforeseen and unexpected consequences elsewhere; a change in one part of a system inevitably has an impact throughout, creating a period of instability until a new, short-term balance has been achieved.

Balance becomes the key and reality an almost impossibly complex relationship between opposing elements: detachment/commitment, love/hate, good/bad, certainty/uncertainty, competition/cooperation, and so on. In attempting to imagine such complexity, it is perhaps more appropriate to think in terms of an *im*balance, in which the constituent parts are always on the point of falling apart but are held in place creatively by the tension between them.

It is rather like trying to imagine Boyle's Law (which states that, at a constant temperature, the volume of a given quantity of gas varies inversely according to the pressure – it works because there is a 'simple' relationship between the three variables) operating with an almost infinite number of dimensions. And, just as it becomes increasingly difficult to conduct an experiment in which either pressure or temperature is taken out of the equation (by reducing them to zero or absolute zero), so everyday life exists somewhere in the middle of the range – a homeostasis that is threatened by extremes. Attempts to produce a society based on 'goodness', for example, which excludes its polar opposite, are doomed to failure.

Thus, 'evil' is not something out there – much as we might try to externalize it on to others – but something that is fundamentally part of each of us. In so far as evil (or the dark side of our natures, characterized by Thanatos, the death wish) triumphs, it has triumphed over each of us – through our apathy, indifference, lack of self-awareness, ignorance or plain selfishness. We have failed to stand up to it. We are implicated, and acknowledging our contribution is the first step towards restoring the fragile balance. The problem is that, in our institutionally dominated world, the opportunities for exercising such personal responsibility are becoming increasingly limited.

The idea of maintaining a 'creative imbalance' does not mean that we should give up the attempt to create a 'fairer', more 'just' or more 'caring' social fabric, but it does mean that we shall have to question just what those concepts mean and what we are really trying to achieve. A 'fairer' society may be less caring because, in our eagerness to be fair, we may turn a blind eye to the hurt this may cause particular individuals who find themselves restricted as a consequence. A more 'just' society may be less than fair as justice is meted out irrespective of individual circumstances. Fairness and justice offer a paradox which can never be resolved in a universal sense. The tension between them can only be used positively when searching for a creative imbalance in particular circumstances and when relating to particular people.

We are dealing with complex interrelationships that are best worked at as close to each individual as possible. It is there that the contradictions and tensions between the various polarities are manifest, where their consequences for others and their impact on the self are most visible, and where there is a chance of change for the better (a definition of growth and development). Again, there is the hint that the way forward lies in the development of local networks of relationships that can tackle such issues in a flexible manner and provide responses that meet the needs of real people. It is also easier to understand why political agendas based on producing a fairer or more equitable society always flounder; it is simply impossible to give expression to such concepts at the global, institutional level. We keep coming back to the notion of 'community' as providing the context within which progress is most likely to be made.

To recognize that there are no universal solutions to life's problems and that each of us must find our own position through our day-to-day negotiations with those around us, is a creative response that both strengthens and enriches the social fabric. Far from being anarchic, such an approach is likely to be surprisingly stable because it is based on establishing shared perceptions of what is important and appropriate. By contrast, the larger and less cohesive the social groupings, the more crude the reactions will be and the greater the impact elsewhere on the social system. As we have seen, the only reasonable response in these circumstances is for everything to become increasingly codified in law and, because it is becoming drawn into areas where the notion of 'right' and 'wrong' cannot be sustained, respect for the law diminishes and further legislation becomes necessary.

The huge bureaucracies that represent order become ever more entrenched in their attempt to keep chaos at bay. Of course, the more successful such moves appear to be, the more likely it becomes that dis-order will break out somewhere unexpected. Just as there comes a point where an increasingly obsessive concern with cleanliness becomes counterproductive and a threat to one's quality of life, it is important to continually acknowledge and celebrate life's messiness if an overreaction is to be avoided; the urge to upset what is the norm and replace it with something that has never been seen or done before is, after all, the source of all creativity.

Life is inherently full of loose ends and we must learn to embrace uncertainty. It is all around us in the form of imprecise language, partial truths and limiting ways of looking at the world, so why not incorporate it into our social structures rather than always trying to fight and contain it? A more flexible, responsive culture is likely to result, one that is more geared to meeting the challenges that lie ahead.

This 'living with uncertainty' also implies an acceptance of the numinous, the unknown and the unknowable. At its most basic, spirituality is being open to the mystery of life, a readiness to listen to the tremors of doubt and anxiety within, as well as the wonder of being at one with creation. To deny that side of one's self is hiding from the terror of not knowing. Like a child who keeps their night-light or cuddly toy into adulthood rather than be alone with their fear of the dark, our preoccupation with order and a purely rational explanation of the material world is a way of sticking our heads in the sand. Materialism and spirituality are polar opposites and, as with all such pairings, a creative imbalance is required. At either extreme they are unhealthy, as can be seen in sects that commit mass suicide, or groups who consume for the sake of consuming while, all around, people starve.

Materialism has been linked with the masculine principle, distinguished by detachment, reason, order, law, competition and hierarchy. Spirituality, on the other hand, relates to the feminine principle, embodying engagement, mystery, nurturing, cooperation and reciprocity. Once again, it is clear where the emphasis in our culture lies. We need to re-establish the balance point. It will be important, for example, to integrate detachment and engagement. To be engaged without detachment risks overcommitment, getting issues out of proportion and losing clarity about what one is trying to achieve. On the other hand, detachment with a lack of engagement leads to superficiality, dilettantism, following false logic and a lack of real impact – all metaphors for a materialist approach that rejects the spiritual.

Spirituality highlights the paradoxes in life rather than the consistencies. It acts as order's foil. To suggest that there is an underlying unity to life while at the same time acknowledging that reality is essentially dualistic – a complex of polar opposites – is profoundly mysterious, more akin to trying to understand how an electron can be both a particle and a wave, rather than accepting that, by means of gravity, two bodies attract one another in a precisely defined way. It requires our attention on several different levels, including both the rational and the intuitive, and results in a 'feel' for the problem rather than a concrete answer that allows us to believe that we understand and have therefore conquered it.

Faith healing has a long history in Russia and, although driven underground during the communist era, has reemerged. It is not unusual for an individual to be both a highly qualified medical practitioner and a shaman. In the fall-out from Chernobyl, many children developed cancers and some interesting research[8] has emerged that shows that, in certain conditions, faith healing is more effective than conventional chemotherapy. This finding is all the more remarkable given that state-of-the-art equipment was rushed to the Ukraine as part of the international aid that was made available. There is a certain symmetry (balance) in the observation that an event as quintessentially material and rational in origin (both symbolic of this world) as Chernobyl should respond to an approach that is altogether non-material and intuitive (symbolic of the other world). Perhaps we are on the point of discovering that the two are not as mutually incompatible as current thinking suggests.

The problem, of course, is that it is very difficult for people to agree on what their spiritual side tells them. The history of the world confirms that consensus about the nature of the great spiritual questions in life has never been achieved and probably never will. To incorporate what are inevitably individual insights into the social fabric is incredibly difficult, and can lead to dogma and intolerance as easily as to an enlightened pursuit of the truth.

National or international religions inevitably create strife, either internally or by creating a sense of 'us' and 'them', and thereby intensify differences. However, the pursuit of spirituality does sit comfortably with a concept of 'community', implying a group of people who are attempting the same journey with open hearts and a willingness both to listen and experience.

Some of the conclusions that were reached earlier regarding the importance of strengthening the links between people who have chosen to relate to one another in some way so that a shared view of what is important may evolve (through the exploration and refinement of language), and collective action be taken to achieve those priorities, begin to form a consistent pattern. Such a coming together of language and action is one constituent of a community. Others will include a membership that is compatible with the insights that evolution has provided regarding effective communication, allowing its processes of decision-making to be correspondingly more complicated (and responsive to individual viewpoints) than any of the systems of involvement that currently exist. Most important will be the creation of an environment in which individuals are more likely both to develop self-awareness and exercise personal responsibility, rather than being swept along by forces they have no hope of controlling. The balance between the individual and the group will be one of the defining features of 'community'; as always, the balance will be delicate.

The concept of 'community' appears to be central to this vision of a future that locates the individual within a network of mutually supportive relationships. It is perhaps symptomatic of how much this side of our experience has atrophied over the past 50 years that the stock of words and phrases we possess to describe community are uniformly confused and lacklustre. We need urgently to establish or rediscover a language that is vibrant and flexible enough to allow us to begin to explore the new world we must create – a language that will give us the confidence to act and produce lasting change. We need to understand what factors combine to create community.

SUMMARY

Language is what makes us human. It is the medium through which we have both come to understand the world around us and to pass that knowledge on to future generations. It is, however, like looking through a fogged glass, one that both distorts and obscures the truth we are seeking. If we are to be in a position to overcome the challenges that await us, we need to be clear about the limitations that language imposes on us.

Those limitations include the inherent tendency for language to be both static and always changing, so that the meanings that attach to particular words and phrases come to take on a different slant. We don't notice the changes because we are part of the evolving culture that causes these subtle shifts. Language is also partial, reflecting the priorities and interests of the age, and certain ideas are therefore easier to explore linguistically than others.

As a result, cultures come to have certain dominant ways of looking at the world and these, by their nature, preclude other, potentially more useful, perspectives. Language scores grooves in the smooth, continuous surface of reality. Tracks become footpaths and eventually turn into motorways down which all human commerce thunders, oblivious of the delights or dangers to either side.

Groupings of all sizes can become monolithic in their beliefs, but such blinkering is obviously more dangerous the more widespread it becomes. Certain institutions generate very fixed ideas of what they are about, and the needs of real people can get lost as a result. Faced by the challenge of another world view, there is a tendency to retreat into one's own mind-set and refuse to look for the assumptions that are at the root of the other's point of view. Many disputes are caused by simple misunderstanding.

Given these limitations, it makes sense to try to minimize them. Distrusting language and always seeking to clarify the meaning that is inherent in communication is a useful starting point. Our decision-making processes will have to reflect the need both to explore meaning and to take the time to produce new meaning, unique to the people involved. Because our views are partial, it will be important to take on board as many perspectives as possible. Above all we must be prepared to change, to move on, and this development will be expressed in changes to the way we use language in everyday life.

It is precisely because of the limitations that are inherent in language and the ways of looking at the world that it gives rise to, that our view of our own nature has changed so much over the centuries. In another hundred years, people's perceptions will have moved on yet again. Our own time is characterized by a belief in what can be summarized as self-development and self-fulfilment that also implies a way of looking at human nature and the processes by which we grow and develop as individuals. It is essentially person-centred in its approach, with the individual occupying centre stage.

One consequence of this emphasis on the individual is a recognition of the importance of the unconscious in how real people and groups behave. A lack of self-awareness is one contributory factor in the way that conflicts develop and, in extreme cases, how unconscious forces can quickly dominate, escalating into episodes of frighteningly mind-less violence. Given the potential for discord on our crowded planet, it is in all our interests that we attempt to under-stand these processes, starting with the way in which we, as individuals, habitually respond to the world.

As with most cultures, however, the commonly held belief systems are not necessarily compatible and, in the scientific viewpoint, we encounter a way of looking at the world that has led to the opposite pole entirely. The harnessing of science to the logic of the institutional world (centrally controlled government initiatives ranging from defence to health, road-building, etc, as well as the multinational corporate drive for new products and greater productivity) has resulted in real people being ignored; at worst, they get in the way and have to be dealt with. Progress must be achieved, whatever the cost.

Science is also a belief system. It assumes a material basis to existence and believes that its approach is the best – in some people's minds, the only way of understanding life and that, in a very real sense, its discoveries are 'the truth'. Its claims are all the stronger for the very real contribution that it has made to changing the human lot. Unfortunately, its way of looking at the world has now reached the stage where it is the major contributor to the problems that we face today. The scientific perspective will remain a valuable and valid one, but we must find an alternative way of looking at the world (a new belief system, in other words) if we are to reverse some of the current trends.

Such a perspective should begin by acknowledging the complexity of life and the fundamental nature of paradox and the particular difficulties that language and our own natures put in the way of our understanding of it. It is a way of looking at the world that is likely to produce organic metaphors rather than mechanical ones and to emphasize the need to search for 'creative imbalance'. As a consequence, we will have to learn to live with uncertainty, trusting our ability to find an appropriate resolution to life's problems. Such solutions will be 'of the moment' and inherently paradoxical; we must be prepared to change our viewpoint in the light of new developments or information. They will focus on ends rather than on means and will imply a continual review of the values that should under-pin the desired outcome.

Clearly, such a way of responding to life is more complex than our current, simple acceptance that most decisions will be made for us in distant centres of power. Only by bringing decision-making as close as possible to the people who are likely to be affected can justice be done to the issues and solutions found that all concerned can own and take forward.

It is a view which presupposes that life has a purpose and that we are part of it, even if we are unable to compre-hend it. That is another belief system, but it is one that is fundamental to the view that places people first and assumes that, if they tackle the problems facing them in an open and honest fashion, they will find a way forward. It also opens us to the numinous – the unknown and the unknowable – and seeks to reassert the balance between spirituality and materialism.

To use these insights to begin to change track and reclaim the future suggests that our perception of our physical environment must change from the static (things) to the dynamic (the interactions and processes that underpin life). As a consequence, the nature of our social relations will shift from exclusion to inclusion, becoming based on trust and mutuality rather than on suspicion and detachment, and our dominant belief systems will continue to promote individuality, but an individuality that is rooted within networks of relationships.

The balance between the individual and the group will be redefined in a way that allows both to prosper. The search for 'community' will lie at the heart of this shift in emphasis. Language and the exploration of meaning in the concepts that this debate throws up will be the medium through which change will be effected.

It is a recipe that offers the possibility of stepping aside from the headlong rush that the global economy has unleashed and begin the process of determining what is important in life and how we can set about weaving a social fabric that secures both the future of our own species and that of the planet as a whole.

We face a simple choice. Either we submit to our individual and collective fates – which, of course, could be either positive or negative in its effects – or we take steps to regain control of our destinies and try to find a way forward that takes our own natures into account. Self-awareness is the key. Understanding how we think about the world and the crucial role of language is a start, but we must convert insight into action if we are to effect lasting change.

Regaining a Sense of Direction

Most people view the prospect of taking a personal stance against the institutional juggernaut with the same enthusiasm that they might exhibit if they were confronted by a battle tank, armed only with sticks. It simply does not seem possible. Surely, they say, we must fight fire with fire. We need legislation that will outlaw speculation, ensure that farming returns to sustainability and creates more local accountability. It is the responsibility of government, not us as individuals.

Although government can clearly help or hinder the struggle to create a more humane society, it should be clear that only a fundamental shift in the way in which we all think about, and act in, the world will be sufficient to break free from our current, disastrous course. At this stage, new laws might create a more aesthetically pleasing tank – brightly coloured, with swathes of flowers around its turret – but they would not alter the nature of the machine. Our increasing dependence on legislation is, after all, one of the main consequences of the way in which currently we perceive reality.

Only a completely different approach to solving what is essentially the problem of being alive will do: a way of acting in the world that relates to the industrial/technological complex in the same way as that did to the feudal system that preceded it (both of which, in their time, provided some kind of answer to the question of how to pursue the good life). And, just as the Industrial Revolution did not spring ready formed on to the social landscape, so we need to begin to create the prototypes of the new age within the body of the old. The Coalbrookdales, and the Abraham Darbys, the Adam Smiths and the Richard Arkwrights are already in our midst if we could but recognize them.

To be sure, the Industrial Revolution could not have happened unless the social and political conditions existed to allow it to take its first tentative steps. Once established, it was unstoppable, but it is clear from experience elsewhere in the world that its emergence was by no means assured. The same is true of the changes that are necessary today. There are many conscious and unconscious forces that will be deployed to prevent them taking place. We should be grateful for, and do our best to support, the quasi democracy that allows us a significant freedom of expression and action. We should also push for the changes that will encourage a local emphasis in all aspects of our lives, but we should not use that commitment to blind us to the need to review and change many aspects of the way that we each personally engage with the world at large.

The nature of language suggests that, if I behave differently, the world is, literally, a different place. By implication, if enough people behave differently, the world will have changed forever and all the structures, ways of organizing social relations and laws that existed before will simply have become redundant. All that will be left will be a shell. Like a factory that has been closed down, the potential to create a product remains, but life has moved elsewhere, leaving the buildings and plant to decay and turn to dust. Ultimately, they will be pulled down and the land will be used in a new and more appropriate way. What once seemed so permanent and impossible to challenge will have been forgotten. Many may mourn the passing of the familiar for a while, but their nostalgia will be transitory as the claims of today take precedence over the memories of yesteryear.

We start the process of significantly changing our behaviour when we begin to look at the world through different eyes. The symbiotic relationship between language and perception begins the subtle shift, altering what we see and the words we use to express our experience. Priorities then change and we do things differently. Thinking and doing have combined in a way that ensures that there is no going back. To think in another way without that transformation being reflected in our actions is to fail to implement the new potential that we embody; to act other than in our habitual ways without pondering on what we have done is to waste energy and miss an opportunity to act consistently and with a sense of purpose.

Language is the key, and trying to evolve a set of concepts that pulls together and moves us on from the jumble of overlapping insights outlined in the previous section is the challenge. From that analysis it should be clear that the aim is not to work out a coherent thought-system (something that becomes fixed and inflexible in its turn), but a way of facing reality that acknowledges the ever-shifting kaleidoscope of impression and interpretation. These are the difficulties that are inherent in being and, by their nature, they are best confronted at the individual level because it is there, and only there, that they are wholly manifest. To continually address the issue of what is best for me and those around me from London, Washington or Brussels is manifestly absurd. The question then becomes, how can we best orientate ourselves towards this new way of thinking about ourselves and the world we inhabit?

We are looking for a new track, leading in a new direction. Inevitably, we have, as yet, only a hazy view of where we want to get and a less than perfect knowledge of the terrain we will have to cross. Worse still, we are encumbered by the assumptions that make following our current course so apparently natural and straightforward. Before we can learn to recognize and name the many rewards and dangers along our new route, we will have to jettison much of the useless baggage that we have accumulated in making sense of where we are now. First and foremost, we will have to recognize just how poorly equipped we are for the expedition. Such humility will be necessary if we are to learn the ways of the world that we are entering quickly enough to save us from the ravages of the one we are leaving.

Just as it is possible to hint at the frailties of our current approaches without comprehensively defining them, so we can suggest the alternative through another four dimensions that indicate how a vicious circle can be changed into a virtuous one. None is new and all are currently being lived and explored in a diverse range of experiments and initiatives up and down the land. It will be in the drawing together of the threads and intertwining them into a strong, consistent skein that will lead us in a different direction entirely.

THE STRENGTH OF PERSONAL RESPONSIBILITY

Imagine that you are driving down the fast lane of a motorway (which probably means that you are exceeding the speed limit!) and you glimpse a figure apparently leaning over a bridge ahead. What do you assume that the person is doing – are they preparing to drop a brick through your windscreen or getting ready to jump? What do you base that assessment on? What can you do about it?

Almost as soon as you have registered the scene, you are beneath the bridge and beyond. It is a scenario that somehow encapsulates life today. The speed, the lack of information, the making of assumptions that cannot be checked, the anonymity and the residual feeling of power-lessness are all around us. Suppose that you later learned that someone – a person you had never heard of, did not even know existed – had indeed committed suicide on that stretch of road. Would you feel a sense of responsibility? You cannot even be sure that the figure you saw and the suicide were one and the same, yet you are perhaps left with the knowledge that you may have witnessed a fellow human being's last, lonely and miserable moments and you could do nothing to help.

Of course, for most of us, these questions probably would not even have risen to consciousness; the awareness of the incident and its possible significance are almost immedi-ately swallowed by the desire to get on and reach our destination, resentful of anything that might slow us down or stand in the way. That obsession with our own business, to the exclusion of all else, is not selfishness or a lack of awareness (although those may contribute) as much as a reasonable and learned response to circumstances in which our ability to influence events is remarkably limited.

The extent to which we are able to exercise personal responsibility (to act morally by accepting responsibility for our actions, or lack of action) seems to diminish by the day. It is not uncommon to feel that your motives are sus-pect in offering help to a stranger or that you are risking life and limb when you give even neutral advice. 'Don't get involved' is the motto of the age.

Integrity is a word that is out of fashion, and one reason may be that it means, at its simplest, 'wholeness'. In human terms, that implies a sense of coherence, consistency and a feeling of being at one with one's self which, in our frag-mented world, is hard to achieve. At best, we present different sides of our character in different circumstances; at worst, we can appear as two, or more, entirely different people. Our expectations about what is acceptable in public and in private can differ markedly, and there is often little link between what we say and what we feel or believe. It is known as 'survival' and we slide from one situation to the next, seeking the line of least resistance.

How often, for example, when we say 'sorry', do we actually mean it? Organizations employ people to deal with complaints (professional 'sorry-sayers') and their function is to soak up the anger and frustration on the other end of the line in an attempt to defuse the situation so that it won't escalate any further – like taking the company to court. The only way to cope in such a job is effectively to divorce what you are saying from what you are feeling. You become skilled at saying sorry in a hundred different ways while you, yourself, remain untouched.

Unfortunately, it is not actually possible to detach your-self in such a way. At some level there is always a connec-tion and to deny it is damaging to your psychic health. Becoming hardened and unfeeling is one consequence and is usually a precursor of burnout. You either cease to be in touch with your real feelings (which has obvious implica-tions for your closest relationships) or you can find yourself overcome with the very remorse that you have been so careful not to reveal to the customer. And the irony is, of course, that you as a person have nothing to feel sorry for; it is the organization that should be feeling the pain.

To a lesser extent, that attempt to control the feeling con-tent of our conversation characterizes every aspect of life today. We have all become skilled at superficial inter-relationships ('have a nice day', 'how are you doing?', etc), but find getting beneath this veneer increasingly difficult (research has shown, for example, that we have fewer close friends than in previous generations).[1] One consequence of continually separating what we say from what we mean is that it becomes harder to hang on to what we do mean – that is, what is important to us. To actually take a stand on anything makes us feel uncomfortable because we are stepping outside our normal blandness and we are unsure how people are going to react. It becomes easier to let things pass until we reach a point where very few things trouble us. We stop questioning why things are the way they are. We cease to be moral agents and any integrity we might have possessed has long since disappeared.

It is a feature of the bureaucratic monoliths that surround us that they are run by rules, and 'going by the book' is another way of avoiding difficult questions about what we ought to be doing in any set of circumstances. 'I was only doing what I was told' has been a justification for malpractice or lack of action down the centuries, but is perhaps more prevalent and less warranted (in view of the general level of education and attitude towards authority) than ever. It also represents a relationship with the external world that is based more on contract than on covenant.

A contract between two parties is designed explicitly to protect and/or entitle one or both parties. It focuses on means rather than on ends and its natural tendency is to limit action that can be taken without mutual consent. A covenant, on the other hand, is an agreement based on mutual trust and goodwill and a desire to work towards a shared goal or vision. It is a joint commitment to set out on a journey, the limits of which may be unclear at the outset. In that sense it is an 'opening up' of potential rather than the 'tying down' that is implicit in a contract.

101

Traditionally, the word 'covenant' had religious over-tones, as in the covenant between God and the Jewish people. The crucial fact about a covenant, however, is that it is based on values, and it is those values that will deter-mine action and behaviour rather than the letter of the law (Jesus of Nazareth's contempt for the Pharisees – the custo-dians of tradition and the law – clearly showed his commit-ment to a way of life that is based on that most fundamental value of all – love).

Most of everyday life is conducted on the basis of cove-nant, with an implicit acceptance of values such as 'good neighbourliness'. Indeed, it is difficult to see how it could be otherwise. Covenant enables rather than restricts, releases time and energy rather than consuming them and emphasizes relationships rather than procedures. It implies reciprocity and a willingness to accept responsibility for one's actions. Daily life would become very difficult on any other basis.

Increasingly, as we have seen, we are moving towards a contract-based culture. The emphasis on 'rights' rather than 'responsibilities' is one aspect of this shift. Rights tend to be guarded jealously (and may have had to be fought for) and to be protected in law – in other words, they are out in the open for all to see, objective, and therefore less depend-ent on the whim and interpretation of the powerful. Responsibilities, on the other hand, are more difficult to pin down. They are inclusive rather than exclusive in the sense that, once accepted, they have ramifications that are difficult to predict. Rights can be sat on – this is my entitle-ment, nothing more, nothing less – whereas responsibilities tend to become meaningless when they are approached in a similar fashion.

The distinction between rights and responsibilities becomes easier to see when the link with contract and covenant is set alongside the characteristics that distinguish the masculine and feminine principles. Comparing the traditional masculine virtues (order, hierarchy, competition, objectivity and compartmentalization) with their feminine counterparts (going with the flow, reciprocity, cooperation, subjectivity and inclusivity) shows the way that things are moving. As already noted, we live in a culture that is dominated by the masculine principle and, in the absence of any corrective measures, it should be no surprise that life is becoming increasingly legalistic and litigious. Such trends will inevitably produce a passive stance towards the world and a consequent reliance on experts to tell us what to do. We need to re-establish the appropriate balance between contract and covenant.

The increasing emphasis on contract is, in part, a reflection of, and response to, the lack of control that people feel. When competing with and doing down your neighbour is seen to be a greater virtue than cooperating with them, contracts at least limit the damage than can be done to you. When it is a question of the weak ranged against the strong, they become a vital bulwark against exploitation and victimization. The paradox, however, is that, in most situations, contracts work best when they don't need to be invoked, when both parties are prepared to operate a degree of give and take – which, in its ultimate form, amounts to a covenant. Once that trust vanishes, the letter of the law becomes the only measure of what is possible, with its attendant restrictive practice, paranoia, soured relations and cheap-mindedness. To imagine everyday life based solely on the drawn out and painful processes of the legal machine is soul-destroying. It is time that we began to agree the ends that we are working towards rather than perpetually disputing the means.

What is pushing us in the direction of legalism is the increasingly fragmented nature of our relationships. Our experience of others tends to be based on their roles – shop worker, teacher, engineer – rather than who they actually are as people. That wouldn't be a problem if we then had time to get to know them in the round, but the reality is that either we never see an individual again or it is in such limited circumstances that getting to know them is not an option. We automatically fill in what we don't know about someone by making assumptions based on appearance, dress and mannerisms. With more and more people we never get past that stage.

Making assumptions is a natural feature of everyday life. When we walk into a room and sit on a chair, we don't check that it is what it appears to be. We see the chair, assume that we know what it is and sit on it. Life would be simply impossible if we had to test everything before committing ourselves. The problem is that our assumptions about people tend to reflect what is going on inside us as much as what is actually happening out there. Whether we like or dislike people, trust them or feel uncomfortable in their presence, often depends on who we are, the circumstances we find ourselves in and how we are feeling.

The more hostile the environment, the more likely we are to feel threatened by others. Our tolerance of a friend who gets drunk in our local bar is likely to be high. Confronted with the same belligerence from a stranger, late at night on a deserted street, however, our response will be very different. In a society that is depersonalized and fragmented, people feel vulnerable and vulnerable people seek protection which, in the absence of anything else, has to be provided by the law and the law-enforcement agencies.

Fragmented social relations lead inevitably to a fragmentation of language, and the increasing incidence of people living in the same town or city using words differently only compounds the problem. 'Difference' becomes something to be wary and distrustful of, rather than a potential asset to be valued for the fresh perspectives it might offer. We retreat ever further into safe enclaves that lead, ultimately, to the walled estates of the super rich – complete with armed security guards – or the complexes that are designed to provide a safe environment for the elderly. A society that is on the run from itself will never find the resources to face up to the problems of life – it can only create even more difficulties.

These trends have nothing to do with actual danger but are a direct reflection of diminishing social cohesion which has an inevitable knock-on effect on our ability to exercise personal responsibility (the ability to sort out our own problems). Once in train, insecurity feeds on itself, an atrophied sense of personal responsibility leading, in turn, to the labelling of whole sections of society as 'different' on the basis of the assumptions that we make about them, which causes us to shy away instinctively from them, further weakening the social fabric.

It is the root of all nationalism, racism, sexism and the other manifestations of the dark side of human nature, and it is really the product of feeling diminished and denigrated by the external world. All the bile of the accumulated slights, rejections and humiliations (real and imagined) that have been heaped on an individual over the years are poured forth on to the other, creating exactly the same sense in them. And so the hatred builds towards inevitable convulsion.

The best defence against mob rule (the coming together of these individual wellsprings of hatred into a universal flood that threatens to drown everyone) is for people to feel in control of their lives, that they are valued for who they are and that, as a consequence, their viewpoint will be respected and given attention. To achieve that, we must be able to exercise personal responsibility in a setting where others are doing the same, where we are each respecting and valuing the other and demonstrating a willingness to take them, as unique individuals, into account in all that we do and say.

It is a measure of how far we have lost control that typically we keep our heads down, obey the rules (in letter, at least), see others in terms of the roles they play, operate on the basis of assumption rather than knowledge, emphasize our rights instead of our responsibilities and accept a situation where appeal to the law is seen as the first, rather than the last, refuge of the aggrieved. The natural consequence is that we feel insecure and vulnerable which, in turn, leads to distrust and suspicion, further fuelling our sense of hazard. It is a vicious circle.

If we are to reverse this trend, to restore a sense of personal responsibility and thus regain control of our lives, the implications are obvious. Starting with those closest to us, we must create the time to get to know them, to understand their hopes and fears and to acknowledge and accept who they truly are. Implicit in that exchange will be the revealing of who we are and the impact that we have on one another, both the positives and the negatives. Many friendships are soured by an unintended hurt and simply fade away because the injury is never acknowledged or expressed. Empathy is required to recognize that there is a problem in the first place, courage and sensitivity to ensure that the issue is approached by both parties in such a way that the situation can be resolved rather than exacerbated. Interpersonal skills are the key and we all need help in refining them.

The object is not to change the other (although that may happen), but to understand and to accept. We may still encounter problems with the untidiness or lack of punctuality of another, but if we understand what these concepts mean to them we may come to see why they give them little importance. Provided our own need for order is also understood and accepted by both of us, it is possible to reach an accommodation where the issues become less important, where behaviours can be seen to complement, rather than oppose, one another. We begin to realize that issues of untidiness/time-keeping only become important when they appear to diminish us by failing to take our needs into account.

Once we realize there is no intention to ignore us as an individual, it is possible to look at issues on their merits – to determine what is 'appropriate' or 'inappropriate'. There are clearly occasions when being on time is more important than others and exercising personal responsibility is about distinguishing between them and acting accordingly (with the person for whom time-keeping is important loosening up in some circumstances and the less punctual individual becoming more reliable in others).

Personal responsibility means accepting responsibility for what we say and do. Clearly it has to start from who we are as individuals, but it must also take others into account and that, in the final analysis, may mean doing things that are, on the face of it, against our best interests. Provided others acknowledge that we are acting in this way and we know that, in other circumstances, they will stand aside for us, we are not diminished but, rather, enhanced. We know that we are contributing to a network of relationships (family, community) that may be greater than us as individuals, but that depends absolutely on our contribution. The creative imbalance between the individual and their wider community is being tested and, in the process, strengthened. It is only when we have to give in and keep on giving in, knowing that no one knows or cares, that the corrosion of self-pity enters the soul.

Trying to understand oneself (gaining self-awareness – that bulwark against the ravages of fate) and others is not an easy process, but through the struggle will come a mutual language that will allow these and any other issues to be explored. The relationship(s) will be the stronger as a consequence (social cohesion will have been increased) and that will provide both the confidence and the basis to extend the process to others. It is the forum in which we most likely will discover the feminine side of our nature and begin to redress the overemphasis of the masculine that pervades our culture.

In time, we will have an orientation to the world that means that we no longer see people merely as roles or objects, but as other beings with whom we wish to engage in a meaningful way. We will no longer unquestioningly obey rules, but seek to understand what they imply – and whether they are relevant – in different circumstances. We will recognize that we have responsibilities and that inevitably these will impinge on others. Exploring the implications of those responsibilities will seem inherently more interesting than insisting on, or campaigning for, our rights. And we will have the confidence to resolve our own problems without having to submit ourselves to the dead hand of the law or rely on the nostrums of so-called experts.

At the very heart of this shift in our perceptions will be the realization that relationships, and their quality, are what make for a decent life.

THE STRENGTH OF CONSENSUS

Decision-making in our society is predominantly authoritarian. That does not mean that people are forced to do things against their will, rather that they accept that others are entitled to make decisions on their behalf, decisions they then obey because it is the law of the land or the rules of the organization. The most extreme example of this acceptance is having one person (the president) who can commit 250 million fellow Americans to war.

If one feature marks out the last hundred years from previous ages, it is not so much the miracles of technology as the sheer number of individuals who now have to be managed if a reasonably ordered society is to exist. Only a little over a century and a half ago, ministers of state were effectively part-time and able to engage in a range of other activities common to their class (a relatively small number of people with a clear sense of identity). Decision-making at all levels was much more integrated into the social fabric. It certainly reflected the prejudices and preoccupations of the time, but it could be seen to encompass and defer to all who held those views.

By comparison, the complexity of government today has created a specialized and ritualized way of dealing with the myriad concerns of its hydra-headed bureaucracy that effectively cuts it off from everyday life. The fragmented nature of society and a lack of clear stratification that might demarcate opinion, mean that political parties now target a computer-created, middle-of-the road voter rather than any flesh-and-blood constituent. An election is about presentation rather than policies and the ministerial team (appointed, not elected) that finds itself in power can claim to have won a mandate for its entire manifesto (not to mention anything else it wishes to enact). The skein of legislature becomes ever more tangled with each promise of reform or modernization, and more and more individuals get caught up in its snares.

The world of corporate business is not much better. Boardrooms across the globe concern themselves with a narrow range of issues that are summed up in the famous 'bottom line'. It is a preoccupation that has much in common with astrology because it concerns a future that is unknown and unknowable. Accountants and managers scour the figures in search of trends that will reassure them that they are on track. Steady growth in sales and profits over many years is the Holy Grail, a proof of good stewardship, even when everyone knows that events on the other side of the globe, a change in legislation or new invention tomorrow, could effectively put the enterprise out of business. Corporate decision-making concerns itself with the grand strategy – what ought to happen on the basis of the information available – while crisis management deals with what actually happens. The workforce is the rough clay from which the vision is fashioned and it has to be worked to produce the shape required; the waste is simply thrown away.

This kind of decision-making assumes that there are leaders (who derive their authority from the position – the roles – they occupy rather than because of who they are as people) and the led (the rest, who usually represent an undefined mass, unknown to the leaders) and that the leaders know best. Faced with the complexity of the reality outlined above, common sense suggests that the only way that this system can function at all is for issues to be simplified and reduced to a few key concepts (such as the 'bottom line'). This inevitably makes decision-making relatively inflexible; how, for example, would a corporation that concluded that relying on the bottom line was not working in its best interests convince others, such as its financial backers, that some totally different measure was appropriate? That is why a social structure based on such decision-making develops a logic and momentum of its own and why, amongst a range of other anti-life tendencies, we find ourselves committed to 'progress' at all costs.

This in-built tendency to oversimplify issues also produces a tendency to polarize them. Any debate becomes a battle for supremacy between the pros and antis of any given position, with the fence-sitters having to come down on one side or the other. Voting is a ritualized way of saying that one or the other must be right, you cannot hold both or another viewpoint entirely. Rather than the discussion being about the merits of each case, the dynamic is often about jockeying for position, judging which way the key players are moving, to ensure that one is on the winning side. The objective becomes to demolish the opposing reasoning rather than testing the validity of one's own.

As Deborah Tannen emphasizes in *The Argument Culture*,[2] our way of engaging with the world has come to reflect the assumption that for any proposition there must be an equally valid opposition (not, you will note, a range of opposing views). The media loves the battle of the sound-bite. People 'win' on the basis of their performance rather than on the strength of their case and far-out interest groups are given legitimacy merely because they offer to 'balance' prevailing assumptions. Reputations are founded on the ability to destroy the opposition. Excitement is in the extremes and the middle ground is viewed as correspondingly uninteresting and dull.

It is an essentially nihilistic stance that rewards aggression and display, traits that, as Tannen suggests, are predominantly masculine; the 'feminine' instinct is to find the basis for agreement within any dispute rather than to exaggerate the differences. If nothing else, we must challenge continually the assumption that there are only two sides to any argument by actively seeking to open up a continuum of options rather than always trying to separate participants into opposing camps.

Looked at in business terms, it is easy to see why the adversarial approach is attractive. A business would see itself as an independent entity. An analogy might be with a steam engine, something with a clear purpose that is seen to be both self-contained and separate from the rest of the world. It is designed and has a hierarchy of functions. In this context, any issue that comes up can be judged by its likely impact on the efficiency of the machine. There is little room for ifs, buts or maybes; it either does or it does not.

The trouble with this comparison is that a steam engine is not separate; it takes raw materials in at one end and pumps out waste products and pollution at the other – if there are too many steam engines, the impact on the environment can be devastating. In other words, simplifying issues by polarizing them may allow our current ways of making decisions to flourish, but they also suggest why they are becoming increasingly counterproductive and beginning to have such a negative impact on life in general. Reality is more complex than we are currently prepared to admit and the challenge is to find ways of moving forward that actively embrace ambiguity and uncertainty.

What is true of business in general becomes positively dangerous in the corporate world. Its impact is global and, as it comes to dominate every aspect of life, its effect on our social environment will be every bit as damaging as that of the Industrial Revolution ever was on our rivers. We cannot see the connections because we are comfortable with a mechanical frame of reference, even though it is now patently failing to mirror the complexity of real life. Only an organic, or systems, approach can do justice to that complexity, stressing, as it does, the interdependence of all aspects of reality and the ways in which it must influence each of us and how, in turn, we can influence it.

When the workings of government are looked at from the same standpoint, the limitations of the mechanistic frame of reference become even clearer; the steam engine analogy simply breaks down completely. The purpose of government is uncertain, and it certainly is not self-contained, affecting the lives of thousands, if not millions, of people with each new piece of legislation (the creation of super states such as Europe will only magnify this tendency).

The oversimplification that is necessary to deal with complex issues such as gay rights, abortion and genetic engineering, let alone find ways to respond to increasing unemployment, control traffic in cities or to set about reducing global pollution and create world stability, means that the differing needs of different individuals are subordinated to the lowest common denominator of coherent – that is, simplistic – legislation. The law has to be black and white, any ambiguities being tested by precedence and appeal until the intention of the lawmakers is generally understood, by which time public perception will have moved on and new laws will be required, setting off the whole process once more. It is easy to see how such an orientation quickly loses touch with reality and points, once again, to the need for a more fluid way of dealing with the balance between order and disorder.

As we have seen, the law is an example of a specialized language in which the meanings ascribed to words may not be the same as those in common usage. By its nature, it is also attempting to minimize the impact of change. When these features are compared with the real world, in which the general fragmentation of society has led to a fragmentation of language and a consequent speeding up of the introduction of new and recycled words, it is easy to see why there is little interest in, or patience for, the legal process.

When neighbours and friends (let alone complete strangers) misunderstand each other and wonder, at times, whether they share the same language, we need processes that interpret one person's point of view to another (rather than attempt to translate them into a third language that neither can understand). Such systems will naturally seek common ground, and thereby bring people closer together, rather than engaging in a win-lose situation that drives them further apart. Social inclusion begins with the attempt to build a common language, not with legislation.

When dealing with the way that people conduct their lives (and that includes almost everything that is currently the concern of government), the principle of personal responsibility suggests that such issues are best dealt with by the people who are directly involved and who have to live with the consequences. It is one of the main themes of this manifesto that the centralized approach to problem-solving actually diminishes the ability of individuals to exercise personal responsibility, with a consequent weakening of the kind of integrity that any society needs if it is to respond to the challenges it will undoubtedly face.

Personal responsibility, however, cannot be exercised in a vacuum and the suggestion that we all need to start by changing the way we relate to those closest to us only takes us so far. Most of the insults and injuries thrown up by everyday life are caused by individuals and situations that we do not know and have little control over. We need to look at how we might extend our sphere of influence by considering other ways of making decisions that include, rather than exclude, people who are likely to be affected by the outcome. The authoritarian approach does not fit the bill and it is worth looking at what other ways of decision-making commonly exist.

Consultation is a favourite, if only because it does not require much from the decision-makers. They decide the issues to be consulted about, and in its most truncated form – the referendum – the way the questions are phrased can guarantee the outcome. The decision-makers usually control the environment in which the issues are discussed and can influence it through publicity, stage-managed events and appeals to loyalty. Finally, they can interpret the result with the added bonus of being able to claim that their conclusion has the approval of the entire organisation, country, etc. In fact, consultation is more often used as a tool to move people towards a decision that has already been taken in principle than as a genuine attempt to influence the outcome of an issue. In that sense, it is more democratic than an approach that says 'I'm the boss and this is what I've decided', but only just.

Consultation can be undertaken with an almost unlimited number of people. True participation becomes increasingly difficult as numbers mount and, with anything above a hundred, is virtually impossible. Participation implies ongoing involvement. It is not a once-and-for-all exercise and implies engagement in a joint enterprise that requires both responsibility for, and commitment to, the outcome. Communication systems, and who controls them, become the key in determining how successful the venture is going to be, with written minutes and reports forming a foundation for member involvement.

The degree of participation varies from committee meetings with fixed agendas and in-built majorities, to less structured groupings who meet to influence and be influenced by common interests. Nevertheless, the reason for the participants coming together is usually defined externally and they have to report to a superior individual or body. There is also usually an in-built hierarchy, with some members having more clout than others by virtue of their position, experience or personality.

All these forms of decision-making imply some degree of external control over the process. That is fine if you happen to be the dominant individual/group but, where exercising personal responsibility is considered important, they pose a problem for those (and that means the majority of us) who happen to be at the wrong end of the process. When you consider that the vast majority of decisions that impact on us as individuals are taken in this way, it is easy to see why personal responsibility is atrophying and why an attitude of doing the best by myself, and hang the rest of you, becomes a reasonable response to life.

Of course, placing control in the hands of others is not of itself a bad thing. Authority can be given to individuals and groups to act on our behalf, provided they are genuinely accountable (and that means our being sufficiently in touch with what they are doing to be able to call them to account). To function effectively, such individuals and groups often have to act in an authoritarian manner, taking decisions without immediate reference to others. It makes no sense for the person who sees children across the road on their way to and from school to consult their charges (or their parents) about the best moment to cross. They have been given that responsibility and, in this case, the way they discharge it is visible to all, which means that action can be taken if they act irresponsibly.

The way in which the apparent paradox of retaining personal responsibility while giving authority to others is resolved, is by involving everyone likely to be affected by the decision in agreeing the parameters within which such authority can be exercised (and by whom), and the manner in which individuals or groups should be accountable. The only way that can be done effectively is through consensus – the bringing together of the parties that are going to be affected by the decisions being taken and reaching an agreement that all are happy with.

No individual or group can be in control because, in choosing to enter the process, each is accepting that the best way to exercise personal responsibility (and come away with that commitment intact) is to embrace uncertainty. There can be no preordained outcome, either implicitly or explicitly, no deals done behind closed doors, just a confidence that a way forward can be found that will embrace everyone's point of view. It is definitely not a question of finding a compromise that somehow balances different, entrenched positions, because it is in the nature of consensus that people's perspectives can and will change, and that something new and positive can emerge from apparent deadlock. A covenant is being struck, indicating a willingness to move forward together into the unknown – a stark contrast to the restrictive practice and 'I know my rights' mentality of our contract-based culture.

It has long been recognized that people contribute different skills to groups. Belbin,[3] for example, ran courses for industry's high-flyers in which randomly formed groups had to solve problems. To his surprise, the groups that might have been predicted to do well – the really top-flight executives – often lost out to groupings of more moderate achievers. Put very simply, he concluded that, to work well, any collection of people needed complementary skills – generating ideas, shaping the process, keeping people motivated and involved, finishing the task, etc; too many team players with one type of skill, or a complete lack of some, and the group becomes merely a number of people acting independently.

Always ready to exploit opportunities to gain a competitive edge, such insights have been adopted by the corporate world. Although consensus and team-building techniques have been effective in non-commercial settings for years (particularly in environmental and community circles), it is time that they had a wider and more everyday application – an understanding of group processes will be vital to the achieving of consensus in whatever context.

Exercising personal responsibility is about being prepared to explore one's own thoughts and feelings, and to listen to those of others. Its hallmarks are a willingness to open up, to be vulnerable and to change. There is an implicit recognition that we are all part of one another, influencing and being influenced. We are not isolated atoms but part of the kind of force-field that is typified by language and the way it evolves. In a group looking for consensus we must use our whole self, from the application of reason to the experiencing of intuition and empathy. The process represents a subtle balance between detachment and engagement.

At its best, consensus implies being 'in community' with those around one. Energy is liberated and it is almost as if the group is functioning on another level. There is a greater sense of each other and of the possibilities each contains. 'I' and 'us' begin to merge and a new multidimensional reality is created in which complexities multiply, but so do awareness and the ability to respond and find a way forward.

Where consensus is operating, there is a continual exploration of the meaning of words, a creative attempt to understand what is being said by framing and reframing statements until there is a mutual understanding of the issues. In the process, the way words are used changes subtlety and this development reflects movement in participants' thinking. The new language represents a new position, one that is different from each individual's starting point, and one that could not have come into existence without the working of consensus.

Consensus also gives as much importance to the experience of reaching agreement as to the words that are being used to frame it. The mood among the participants may be more important than what is being said, and more time may be spent trying to understand what is happening than in discussing the matters that have ostensibly brought people together. Guided fantasies, working on a group myth, improvizations and the exploration of dreams may all help to identify the real issues that have to be resolved. Progress can be elusive and it is often a question of waiting for the moment when everyone present can 'feel' (or even 'see') the problem and contribute to its solution. In the same way that an artist knows when a painting is finished, so a sense of completeness will suggest that the necessary work has been done and it is time to move on.

Given that we imbue life with meaning through the ways we habitually think about the world, the idea of potentially having to set such familiar patterns aside to achieve consensus can appear daunting, rather like walking naked into a room of strangers. Firstly, it is worth reflecting that our world views are rarely static. We are continually amending and updating them in the light of experience. Where we do find ourselves digging our heels in and resisting the pressure of change, it is often because we have a prejudice, a viewpoint that we are not prepared to examine closely because it reflects, or stems from, some aspect of our psyche that we are unaware of or are uncomfortable with. Prejudices are rarely positive in our lives and when consensus challenges them, or forces us to face what lies behind them, it is doing us a service, painful though it may be at the time. We are being given the opportunity to grow as an individual.

Secondly, consensus assumes that everyone has a valued contribution to make and that, provided we are truly speaking for ourselves (and not rehearsing some political tract or giving voice to a prejudice), our views are worth listening to. The objective is not to convert everyone to a particular viewpoint, but rather to utilize the wisdom within the group to find a more appropriate solution to a problem than would be the case if it were left to a single leader or small élite.

That wisdom is to be found in surprising places. It is not necessarily the articulate who have the greatest impact. Often it is the individuals who are silent who are struggling deepest with the issues and need the greatest encouragement both to recognize that their inner conflict is valuable and to give voice to what is concerning them. It is through paradox and the struggle to resolve the apparent contradiction between different points of view that true progress can be made.

Thirdly, the clearer the participants are about the values they believe should underpin the issues being discussed, the easier it is to reach consensus. Arguments in everyday life can usually be traced to the participants starting from different assumptions, with a stage being reached where it is acknowledged, implicitly or explicitly, that a redefinition of the problem has occurred and some kind of accommodation has been reached. By clarifying principles at the outset, not only does the process start off with agreement rather than dispute, but a joint position offers a reference point when the going gets tough.

While there may be considerable debate about emphasis, it is rare for a major clash on values to occur because, ultimately, they can be traced back to what we can all agree is important in life. The search for consensus starts off by building a foundation that everyone can subscribe to so that, rather than the person who shouts loudest or persists the longest winning the day, it is possible to keep returning to basics and asking how the differing positions reflect the set of agreed principles. Sometimes the principles will need to be extended or clarified; more often, the preferred option suggests itself. Consensus is a process based on the presumption that agreement is possible.

Fourthly, although it can work perfectly well with strangers, consensus works best within a group of people who know and trust one another and who have a joint purpose in being together beyond the desire to explore the workings of consensus. Being familiar with others can create problems. It is a common enough experience in the workplace to attend meetings where certain subjects are simply not raised because everyone knows that, if they are, one or more members will become defensive, pull rank, get their own back at some future date or otherwise prevent open discussion; experience has shown that it is just not worth the effort and the group is the poorer as a consequence.

If people are open to the possibility of consensus, however, knowing each other well allows ever deeper levels of meaning to be explored. Prejudices, insecurities and personal sensitivities become the raw materials through which the process unfolds and everyone has an interest in supporting and encouraging the pursuit of increasing clarity and personal growth. Accepting personal responsibility for one's contribution to helping another through the pain of change will minimize the dangers of any one individual feeling rejected, devalued or cast adrift, as well as providing a learning opportunity for oneself. It is a virtuous circle and one that becomes increasingly sophisticated over time.

Finally, while consensus seeks to find a way that is true to the people involved, that is not the same as finding the truth. For all the reasons discussed above, our view of reality will always be partial, always distorted by the particular lens that is us. As a consequence, any agreement that has been reached is only as good as the level of mutual understanding about what that agreement represents in practice; it is an 'outcome of the moment', a new 'creative imbalance'. Such understanding will begin to unravel and fragment the moment the meeting breaks up. As members disperse and get on with life, their courses are diverging literally and metaphorically. Their priorities, perspectives and interests reassert themselves and the unfolding of meaning in each life continues separately.

Imperceptibly at first, but then with ever-widening effect, the words that form the substance of what was agreed begin to mean different things to different people. For that reason, what is agreed through consensus can never be a once-and-for-all statement of what is considered to be important. At the very least, there will need to be periodic reviews of what the words actually mean and whether they are still relevant to the issues under consideration. More often than not, a new form of words will be appropriate, reflecting a change of perception or a deepening of understanding.

The seeking of consensus can be time-consuming and is clearly not appropriate for all decisions. The key is to recognize those areas where consensus is needed and where it might actually get in the way of action being taken – which, after all, is the objective of decision-making processes, to ensure that appropriate action follows. It will also be important to tie the various approaches together, so that there is a clear understanding, achieved through consensus, of the limits of action that individuals and subgroups can make on their own behalf or that of the whole, and how they are to remain accountable. In other words, the full range of decision-making options – consensus, participation, consultation and authoritarian – are available; it is a question of ensuring that the right combination is chosen for a particular issue.

A considerable body of work exists about the workings of consensus. Organizations such as the Institute of Cultural Affairs and the Foundation for Community Encouragement have evolved techniques by which groups can be guided towards consensus.[4,5] Other organizations exploring similar themes would include the New Economics Foundation, InterAct, the Environment Council's Environmental Resolve programme, Mediation UK, etc.[6]

The growth in Peace Studies reflects a growing interest in trying to bring together factions whose interests appear diametrically opposite and find common ground. Charismatic individuals such as Dee Hock have used techniques that were originally evolved to make businesses more profitable to find solutions to long-standing problems such as the over-harvesting of the fisheries in the Gulf of Maine.[7]

Such techniques fundamentally look to break entrenched positions by searching for a new definition (or redefinition) of the issues that everyone can fall in behind. By recognizing what they have in common, such as the future of the planet, even long-standing enemies can find ways of moving forward together. If consensus in a cold climate is possible, how much more likely it is to flourish in more hospitable surroundings.

To see how far we have come in the discussion so far, it is worth contrasting some of the differences between consensus and the general way of thinking and making decisions based on the rational, or scientific, method. The application of objectivity to a problem, breaking it down into its constituent parts to understand the whole, has become such a dominant way of looking at the world that consciously or unconsciously we like to think that we apply its cool rationality to almost every situation we face (our hierarchical, bureaucratic systems are a perfect analogy of the approach).

Despite all the evidence that, in most everyday situations, that is not what we actually do and, when we do, the result is often a compounding of the problem, the belief that there is an answer to every problem persists in boardroom and Cabinet office alike. It is a mechanistic view of life - if 'a' equals 'b' and 'b' equals 'c', then 'a' must equal 'c', end of story. There can only be one right approach and every other perspective must, by implication, be wrong.

The problem, of course, is knowing which is the right approach, and the traditional scientific method relies on the building up of a body of evidence that supports a particular theory. The greater the evidence, the stronger the theory. This building-block approach is fine when the edifice is growing in a manageable way, but it begins to break down completely when new problems and hypotheses are being thrown up on an almost daily basis. There simply is not the time to test anything adequately and, as a consequence, the emphasis is on destroying any aspect of the evidence that supports a particular theory or strategy in the hope of terminally weakening the whole structure, before rushing on to the next.

If you have to be either for something or against it, it is often easier to be against it. That is particularly true of what are called 'social policy issues', where the spotlight of media attention is constantly redefining the issue of the moment and providing the oxygen of publicity to the army of detractors clamouring to spike the guns of any minister who is brave enough to launch a policy initiative. And when the results are not those predicted, as inevitably they are not because circumstances have changed, the world is full of pundits saying 'I told you so'.

By contrast, consensus is essentially an organic approach that looks at things in the round and evolves towards a preferred position with an assumption that, sooner or later, it will be appropriate to move on yet again. There are no 'winners' and 'losers' because everyone owns the outcome and sees in it the best possibility of improvement both for themselves and others. When things don't turn out as expected, there is no point in trying to apportion blame because it belongs in equal measure to everyone. In such circumstances, the emphasis is more likely to be on trying to find the new way forward together than on wasting time on recrimination.

The scientific method is a very powerful tool in limited circumstances. One of the problems we face as a society is that we have based our whole approach to life on it. Consensus offers us an opportunity to establish a way of decision-making that is more in step with the kind of reality that affects the everyday interactions of people.

THE STRENGTH OF LOCAL ECONOMIES

In *News from Nowhere* (1891), William Morris looked to a time when money had disappeared. Markets existed as convenient points for people to find anything they might need, but no cash changed hands. Things were made for the love of making them and, as a consequence, they were made to astonishingly high standards. In a sublime balancing of supply and demand, you could always find what you wanted because idleness was unknown and craftspeople were forever varying what they made to avoid becoming stuck in a rut. Even if you lost something, it did not matter because you could always get a replacement, and the person who found the lost article would use it themselves or return it to the market for someone else to pick up. And, because goods were freely available, no one was tempted to take more than they needed.

Of course, it was a utopian dream. As far as we can tell from recorded history, there has always been a call for some medium of exchange, implicit or explicit. Ownership – and with it the right to dispose of what one owned – came early and naturally to humankind. Within a family or group, goods and services might be shared, but it was invariably on some understood basis of privilege; your share depended on your place. When groups bartered, there was an assumption that both parties would attempt to secure the best deal for themselves and there was usually an implicit notion of value against which to judge one's success. That tension between parties, that desire to make on a deal, now explicitly underlies the money economy. It has become the sole purpose of the marketplace and is reflected in each stage of the process between producer and purchaser.

Just because William Morris' dream was utopian does not mean that we have to accept the monetary system as it is. His vision at least put the needs of real people at the heart of the transaction, and that surely must be the measure of how well an economy is functioning. Economics is not an end in itself, but a way in which people can improve the quality of their lives (which is not the same thing as acquiring wealth). We have seen how the global economy rides roughshod over whole communities in the pursuit of profit and is becoming increasingly abstract as billions of dollars rush around the world at the touch of a computer key. It has lost all sense of being about people and can thus be seen to be failing in the most basic test of how an economy is performing.

Although it is far and away the largest source of economic activity in the world today, the global money economy is by no means the only one. Barter still exists, both at the corporate level (with deals being struck in terms of commodities rather than money) and locally (with individuals engaged in long-standing understandings about offering one another goods and services that never touch the mainstream economy). Many national corporations, either individually or by cooperating together, offer loyalty cards that customers can use to purchase goods directly from the organization or elsewhere. Vouchers clipped out of magazines are another variation on this theme of parallel economies.

The idea of a local currency does not appear quite so strange or novel when seen alongside the diversity of systems that are already in existence. What a local economy offers, however, is loyalty to a community. It also offers a degree of protection against the vagaries of the global marketplace where, at the touch of a few computer keys, entire regions can find themselves deprived of the very thing that makes the world go round; money becomes scarce and people's quality of life suffers as a consequence. Creating a local economy not only means that trading can continue in a recession, it also means that, over time, the area covered becomes less dependent on goods and services coming in from outside.

The development of local economies is something of a growth industry, with new examples springing up in the most unlikely places. Details of some of the more established schemes are given below, but, for the present, it is worth concentrating on the features that are likely to give local economies such a significant role in the promotion of personal responsibility and consensus, and thereby contribute to the creation of 'community'.

Just as ongoing trading across continents leads to the development of relationships between the people who are engaged in the activity, so trading at a local level cements the links between people within a community, the major difference being that local people are likely to see one another when they are not trading and so relationships are potentially further reinforced. In fact, trading becomes a mechanism by which relationships can be fostered and sustained. You can get to know people through trading in a way that encourages the growth of personal responsibility.

In a local economy, relationships between people who trade are very different from those in the mainstream economy. When we go into a superstore, we are motivated solely by getting the best deal we can for the money we are prepared to spend. We are not interested in the sales assistants who serve us or the circumstances in which the product we are buying was produced. By contrast, local trading introduces an element of negotiation between the parties, a clarification of what exactly the provider is offering and what it is that the purchaser wants. A personal deal is struck.

In the process, we are likely to learn more about the person we are involved with, their hopes and disappointments, their reasons for choosing to offer that particular skill, and so on. We begin to see them as a real person and, as a consequence, we are able to exercise personal responsibility in the way we arrange the deal; their personal circumstances become one of the issues we consider in deciding whether and how to proceed.

As we have seen, the more we get the opportunity to exercise personal responsibility, the more likely it is that we will come to understand both ourselves and those around us. We will gain a better sense of who we are and, as a consequence, become more open to consensus as a decision-making process. Our confidence in ourselves and others will become such that we can begin to feel comfortable with uncertainty and accept that our own perceptions, and sense of what is important, will inevitably change. It is an incremental process, a gradual strengthening of our abilities to map out and share a common view of what is important.

Trading locally also rewards skills that the wider economy simply fails to recognize. Most of the work we undertake is not paid for and, in that sense, is not rewarded. From cooking meals to helping someone move house, from do-it-yourself to gardening, the myriad jobs we do for ourselves and those closest to us are barely seen as being work. Yet people employed by organizations and paid to do exactly those same things would see what they are doing as contributing just as much to the economy as an accountant or lawyer.

In a local economy, work that is currently unpaid can potentially reach a far wider audience. The person who enjoys making curtains is no longer restricted to the windows in their own home or those of friends and neighbours, and demand for their work could even reach the stage where it develops into a small business, several people working alongside one another, with the same or complementary skills.

The important thing is that our curtain-maker should be free do to as much or as little as they want. We currently equate 'real' work with employment and employment should, ideally, be full-time. Because a local economy can be used to trade anything that people both have and want, each individual can develop a range of marketable skills. It does not have to be a 'business' and, as a consequence, work allows an opening out of potential, compared to the closing down that happens in the mainstream economy where the development of one's talents is determined by the job one does, leaving whole areas of one's being unknown and unexplored.

And, because a local economy permits a single trade (compared with the mainstream economy where a registered company and an office, shop or factory are required almost as soon as you start trading), it is easier for people to experiment, to see if they have the skills to offer something on a wider basis, and whether they enjoy it sufficiently to want to extend their competence. A framework has been created that allows individuals to express themselves in all their variety (self-realization) and rewards them for their industry, providing a sense of achievement in having contributed something that others want and a system of exchange through which they can meet their own needs – which is not so very far from William Morris' vision after all!

It is also easier to work alongside people who already have the skills (by paying them for their time in local currency) and to learn in a more relaxed, domestic environment. There is less threat of the teacher losing out to their pupil because, if the latter does come to demonstrate greater skill than the former and be in greater demand, that does not automatically mean the loss of all their business. They may have to re-evaluate their position and develop other skills, but that is an opportunity for change and personal growth.

Individuals are less likely to spend a lifetime pursuing one interest (although they might if this specialization were a true reflection of who they were – an artist, for example, in the widest sense of that word, is someone who develops by pursuing a single theme throughout their life) but to explore new possibilities continually and to change the balance between the various activities they are undertaking. Because the emphasis will be on wholeness – experiencing life in all its aspects – it is also probable that work will take on a seasonal cycle, reflecting a more natural rhythm to life and putting us back in touch with the natural world. This change, in turn, will be reflected in the development of language; we might rediscover the Romantics' love of nature and become more rooted in it.

Ultimately, a local economy allows people to enjoy what they are doing because they have chosen how much of a particular sort of work they wish to do, as well as when and where they will undertake it. In short, it leaves people in control, which is the basis for the exercise of personal responsibility. Because they are committed to what they are doing, the results are likely to be of better quality and more durable than the fruits of mass production. It is not too far fetched to say that they will contain more love.

The closer the producer and purchaser are, the more love will be part of the transaction. Preparing and serving a meal is symbolic in many ways, but giving and sharing are at its heart. It is a traditional way in which people express love, cooking food that they know the recipient will like, and taking extra care with both the dishes and their presentation. In the same way, making something with a particular individual in mind is both more likely to strengthen the link between the two and to ensure that more thought and feeling go into the finished article.

Any economy should be judged on its ability to meet real human needs (including personal development) and we must ensure that the workings of our local economy do not disadvantage some individuals at the expense of others. One of the features of the mainstream economy is that there is a huge differential in earnings between the individuals who participate in it. A commodity trader can make millions on a single deal, while a person looking after elderly people has a continual struggle to keep their head above water. Such differentials are no reflection of the people involved as people, nor do they relate to the value of the jobs being done; they are institutional, which is to say that they reflect market forces that just happen to fall out that way.

The consequence of these imbalances is that the commodity trader has many more options than the carer. The commodity trader will probably have more leisure time and they certainly have access to a wider range of cultural, recreational and educational opportunities than the carer. The commodity trader will have more influence in the decision-making processes and, by being able to employ paid experts such as lawyers, etc, will feel more in control of their life – and all because their work is valued differentially.

By standing that principle on its head and saying that all work in a local economy should be valued equally, we will be going some way to giving each individual the opportunity to develop their skills on an equal playing-field – that is, they don't have to make a choice about what to do based on the best return – and to give them all access to roughly the same resources to purchase whatever goods and services they require. More importantly, they will be able to engage in consensus as equals, with the consequence that a person's contribution will be valued for its wisdom and veracity rather than for the amount of money they have been able to amass.

The fact that there are only 24 hours in a day is a great leveller if everyone is paid at the same hourly rate (called simply 'an hour for an hour'). Of course, people are not equal in how hard or quickly they work, or in their ability to sell themselves to others or even in the talents they possess, but everyone has a range of activities that they enjoy doing and we are all sufficiently different to ensure that what I take delight in will be something someone else will be more than happy to leave to me because they themselves cannot do it or hate doing it. A local economy celebrates difference and makes it a virtue. The mainstream economy, because of its size, seeks to standardize everything and squeeze out the individual element.

It will be argued that real life is far too complicated to be contained within the simple framework of 'an hour for an hour'. How can it embrace the differences that obviously exist between a surgeon or microchip designer and a road-sweeper? Some activities require an extensive apprenticeship and/or preparation work before an hour's package can be delivered, others are aimed primarily at groups rather than single individuals; some can only be done for short periods and yet others involve processes and materials that are hard to quantify in this way.

These are all complications but are not impossible to resolve. They are handled quite adequately in the money economy by separating costs into 'labour' and 'materials', or including elements for less tangible inputs. Transparency will be critical, allowing potential purchasers to see how the price is made up and providing choices about the quality of the materials to be used, and so on. What they should also be able to check is that one producer is not charging more than the hourly rate for their time.

The mechanisms are not complicated and, with a little ingenuity, they can be applied to any situation. All that is being suggested is that the principle underlying any negotiation about trading should be changed to reflect the fact that it is an individual's time that is being valued rather than some artificial notion of scarcity or profitability. Preparation time could be legitimately included and, on the basis of charging a fixed amount for an hour's work, the cost of a service to each member of a group that received it would be calculated by the number of hours delivered divided by the number of participants.

Taken together, these features are what distinguish a local currency from the wider, money economy. It is for the benefit of, and controlled by, the people it is designed to service (who do not have to comprise a community as such; they could exist on the Internet as members of a global club trading specialist items). It is available when needed. Any wealth created is retained within the group/community rather than disappearing elsewhere, and anything that people have to offer that others want is recognized and valued. The unit of exchange is based on time and any individual's capacity to earn and spend is roughly the same as everyone else's; mutuality is not distorted by the effects of significant wealth differentials. In other words, it is an economy that assists the meeting of human needs rather than creating a framework of 'haves' and 'have nots'. As a consequence it is less likely to lead to a distorted view of what we actually want and what is important in life.

As indicated above, local economies are mushrooming all over the place and an extensive commentary (both academic and popular) is available. Thus far, we have been examining ends rather than means and it is worth sketching how a local economy works in practice. There are many examples in existence, including Local Exchange Trading Systems (LETS), Time Dollars, Romas and Ithaca Hours. The emphasis of each is different: Ithaca Hours, for example, issue a physical currency, LETS systems do not – cheques are exchanged for goods and services and then balanced centrally as in a conventional bank. These are early days in the development of local currencies and each approach has both its merits and its advocates. However, the most widespread system at present is LETS and it will stand as an example of the kinds of practical issues that have to be addressed.

The primary challenge facing all local currencies is credit – how it is created and then controlled. If we call our community currency 'hopefuls', then, in a LETS system, the sum total of all the 'hopefuls' in circulation will be zero. In other words, at any one time, there will be roughly the same number of people in debt as there are in credit. In that sense, being in debt (or 'commitment' as it tends to be called) is positive, because it encourages trading. I don't actually have to possess any 'hopefuls' to meet a need I may have. Credit is immediate and stimulates the local economy (whose performance is usually measured in terms of the number of transactions taking place in a given period). By going into commitment I am also increasing the balance of the person I am trading with, which may stimulate them to go out and buy something.

If I keep on going into commitment, however, I may be meeting my needs but I am contributing nothing to the community – I am getting rich at its expense. In most communities, people would be motivated to participate and would pass backwards and forwards continually through 'zero'. There is, nevertheless, always the danger of stagnation. I may not wish to go further into commitment, but find myself unable, for whatever reasons, to trade and thus to bring my account back into balance, so I do nothing. Sitting on a lot of 'hopefuls' and not trading also puts a brake on the system, tying up resources that could be used to increase the wealth of the community.

The way to avoid this difficulty is transparency. All members of a LETS scheme have access to each other's balances and trading history (a trading history that shows a person having traded several times the amount they are currently in commitment suggests that they are more than able to get back into credit). If individuals appear to be stuck, others can make a point of trading with them, or of seeking other ways in which the situation can be ameliorated. If there is a question over an individual's commitment to the system, that will soon show up and steps can be taken to remedy the situation. Transparency also sits comfortably with the principles that underlie personal responsibility and consensus.

There are many tasks that need to be done that do not fit into a straightforward individual-to-individual trade. A community will have to undertake maintenance, cleaning and day-to-day running of many communal facilities, from libraries, educational and health centres (although what these might look like in a community setting is a subject in itself),[8] to roads and parks, if it is to accept full responsibility for its destiny. A local economy can provide the means through the raising of what are effectively local taxes. Put another way, individuals within the community are committing themselves to contribute an agreed number of hours a month/year to using their talents directly for the benefit of the community or paying others to use theirs.

The ends to which these 'taxes' should be put, and therefore the amount of hours that will have to be found by the community as a whole, is a matter for everyone to agree through the mechanisms of consensus. Individuals, or small groups, might then be delegated to administer the community fund in specified areas, through engaging people to do the agreed task by negotiating a trade in the usual way (the type and quality of work required and the time it will take).

The emphasis must always be on trading. The more trading that takes place, the richer both individuals and community will become – and it is a wealth that is real because it reflects what people actually want. Local economies can exist totally independently of the mainstream economy and that may be a long-term goal but, at present, the majority of our needs will still have to be met in dollars and euros. By encouraging conventional enterprises into the local economy, not only do our 'hopefuls' go further, they can potentially even increase the turnover and profitability of the participating businesses (the conventional measures of success and ones that, in the fullness of time, will be replaced by concepts such as promoting self-awareness and self-realization and increasing the wealth of the community).

Local shops that offer a percentage of sales in 'hopefuls' may initially be doing no more than offering a discount in another way (instead of vouchers, loyalty points, special offers, etc.), but they are engaging with their community in an entirely different way and will gain customer loyalty as a consequence (perhaps coaxing people back from the supermarkets). In time, they may recognize that it is in their interests to increase the proportion payable in 'hopefuls' because they can pay an element of wages for any staff recruited in the neighbourhood; local income can also be spent on repairs and decoration, and improving and maintaining the immediate environment to make the premises more attractive. Income can even be used to access the services of local professionals such as lawyers and accountants.

In the same way, large-scale landlords, such as local authorities and housing associations, could charge an element of rent in local currency and spend it to encourage local people to become involved in the repair and maintenance of their homes, and the upkeep of the surrounding area. It is another way of giving control back to individuals and communities, and there is growing evidence that these kinds of initiatives lead to a reduction in crime and vandalism. They can only strengthen the sense of community, of belonging to and identifying with a particular area.

The more a community can meet its own basic needs, the more in control of its destiny it will be. There are plenty of goods and services that will still have to come from outside, either because the raw materials do not exist within or because certain skills and processes are not available; it is unlikely, for instance, that every community will have access to a competent furniture-maker. The basis on which such trade would be conducted, however, would be very different from a simple pursuit of profit (see below). Particularly talented individuals might be known and in demand over a wide area but, in general, it is likely that any needs that could not be met within a community would be satisfied as close to home as possible.

One of the traditional features of the current money economy is to allow funds accumulated in one part of the market to be invested in another where resources are more scarce or returns greater. It is a mechanism that allows things to happen that would otherwise have failed through lack of capital or cash-flow problems. As we have seen, however, debt and the servicing of debt have come to dominate the money economy. Quite simply, the whole edifice would collapse if growth, which is based on the lending of money, stopped (with catastrophic consequences for us all).

We already recognize that growth cannot continue indefinitely, if only because the earth has finite resources, but we have to go on behaving as if that were our goal. We also recognize that investment and growth in the economy are not necessarily, or even often, reflected in quality of life as experienced by ordinary people. The building of office blocks, motorways, factories, and so on brings very mixed blessings to those living close by. An economy that is actively seeking to enhance quality of life rather than to create a return on capital is therefore likely to focus on different, more immediately human, outcomes.

Within a local economy, 'capital' can be raised by allowing individuals and groups to go into commitment. Because there are always people in commitment/debt and being in commitment is natural and healthy, it is a normal part of the way that such an economy functions. To support a project that implies going into significant commitment is thus only an extension of the basic principle. It could potentially skew the whole economy, however, and any such proposal would have to be agreed by the community as a whole. Working through consensus, members would have to satisfy themselves as to the ethics of the scheme as well as the integrity and capabilities, amongst other things, of its proposers. It is an altogether more healthy way of determining priorities than making decisions that are based on the single indicator of how much return a particular investment is likely to produce. Everyone potentially affected by the project will be able to have their say rather than the few people who have, or manage, money.

Implicit in this approach is a recognition that the current distinction between 'home' and 'work' will begin to disappear. Not only would people, for the most part, utilize their skills within their immediate community, the accommodation they need will come to reflect the activities they are undertaking; a workshop might require more space than a kitchen. Larger production processes or specialized functions (high-tech, dockyards, and so on) may become communities, or a collection of communities, in their own right (although putting all one's eggs in one basket has traditionally been considered a risky ploy and one would expect some diversification, if only to the production of food, as self-protection). Communities might form around a manufacturing process such as the fabrication of computers, for example, and provide a regional service.

Individuals and groups involved in making a common product (software design, for example) would also share a community of interest and might set up virtual communities (with their own virtual currencies) to trade information, access spare parts, and so on. There would be an openness about exchanging ideas and processes that is totally absent in today's atmosphere of carefully guarded industrial secrecy because the incentive to grow and make ever larger amounts of money would no longer exist. Only through genuine partnership (across communities) could progress be maximized.

A small-scale, cooperatively run manufactory might be considered an important asset for the locality, but its ability to produce goods at a profit, and thus to produce a return on the investment being made, would not be a consideration. By investing in one's own community, one is looking primarily to improve its long-term viability and quality. The impact that such a structure might have on the area – socially, morally, ecologically, aesthetically – becomes a priority as well as the relationships between the people working in it (and what investment in terms of time, energy and skill they are prepared to make to get it up and running).

To 'invest' significantly in any one initiative (which might also include improved housing, leisure facilities, and so on) would be a serious step, but the advantage would be that a long-term asset is acquired for no more than the sweat on people's brows. The need for an injection of capital from outside, with the consequent draining away of wealth to others and the ever-present danger of having the plug pulled if better returns can be realized elsewhere, would have been avoided.

A local currency offers a wonderfully flexible way of meeting need; it encourages openness in relationships, and it implies the continuing involvement of everyone in how the economy is developing and the priorities that are to be pursued.

THE STRENGTH OF COMMUNITY

Personal responsibility, consensus and local currencies are the cornerstones of community. One of the central issues of human existence is the relationship between the individual and the group, and they offer ways of looking at the creative imbalance between the self and the other that provides the potential for a win-win outcome for both. In an individualistic society (where the self is seen as primary) the individual is ultimately the loser because they become increasingly isolated and vulnerable in the mass. In a communistic society (where the needs of all the 'others' take precedence over the individual), the community loses out because initiative is stifled.

It is important to recognize that 'communal' and 'community' are not synonymous. Community is the more general word, capable of embracing both communal living (the sharing of living space, possessions and style of life) and a group of individuals who choose to cooperate for a specific purpose at a specific time. It is a way of looking at the relationship between self and other that does not preclude either pole, but is generally concerned with negotiating the middle ground, defining and debating the point at which what is properly private becomes public.

Another way of looking at community is to recognize that it represents the balance between freedom and equality. If freedom is taken as the freedom to do whatever I want irrespective of the consequences for others, the outcome is inevitably the survival of the strongest and the emergence of a set of social relations based on force and violence. If equality is taken to mean the limiting of what I can do in the interests of ensuring that everyone is treated the same, the result is a tyranny based on rules and peer group pressure. In neither is the individual truly able to flourish in the sense that they can realize their own unique potential as a person. The wider community is the poorer as a consequence.

A creative imbalance between freedom and equality is required and, if it is to be both achieved and maintained (ideally through consensus), it has to be worked at. That means evolving a set of concepts (a language) that identifies the issues that have to be balanced, and a way of looking at what is happening in practice (feedback) that will allow adjustments to be made and a new equilibrium to be achieved, always recognizing that nothing lasts forever and that, sooner or later, any agreement must be renegotiated and a new set of priorities put in place.

The problem we face as a society is that such a conceptual framework simply does not exist. The key ideas of freedom, equality, community, democracy, and so on have become so debased as to be virtually meaningless. 'Freedom' becomes the opportunity to drive a certain brand of car, 'equality' is about demanding paper rights, 'community' is something we think we have lost and look back to with nostalgia, while 'democracy' is regarded so cynically that even voting becomes a meaningless chore that is only exercised if there is nothing good on the television. That is the cancer at the heart of our society; the lack of clarity about issues that are of vital importance to the well-being of each of us, as well as the societies we inhabit, is what allows the continuing development of the global economy, the growth of agribusiness, the institutionalization of life and the worship of individualism.

Only by developing a coherent vision that puts meaning back into these concepts can we begin to rebuild a world that is staring catastrophe in the face. An obvious starting point is to go back to basics and focus on our perceptions of what it means to be human. And it must be emphasized that it is *our* perceptions – a century hence and many of those perceptions will probably seem as quaint as the idea that you can tell personality from bumps on the head. In so far as we have a coherent view of human nature, it can be summed up in the phrase 'self-realization'.

To believe that it is part of each individual's purpose to strive to realize themself has implications for the concepts of freedom and equality. 'Freedom' becomes, simply, the freedom to realize one's self, and 'equality' is then that freedom extended in equal measure to all. Immediately the concepts have both limits and a sense of interrelatedness rather than mutual incompatibility.

When looked at on the personal level, it is possible to envisage a process of negotiation between individuals that ultimately benefits both parties. The search for consensus leads to new perspectives and a sense of going forward together rather than being in competition with one another. In fact, it is but a short step to recognize that to move towards self-realization actually requires other people engaged in the same process. The more attuned and sensitive those involved are (a balance of intuition and reason) to the needs of both self and other, the more likely it is that growth and development will occur for both.

There is a clear parallel with child-rearing. A child cannot grow in a vacuum; it needs the presence of others who are actively interested in and wish to promote its welfare. Some parents may be more gifted in terms of intelligence, understanding, resources, and so on, and that may have an impact on their child's development, but the critical factor is the strength of the bond between adult(s) and child. We use the term 'love' to describe that deep and total engagement with another human being, and the mother–child relationship has often been portrayed as being the most perfect expression of our human capacity for love. The 'falling in love' of two people is likewise treated with reverence as a mystery (when two become one) that lies at the heart of existence. Clearly, love operates in an analogous way to a force field, blurring the boundaries between self and other.

These two examples are not somehow separate from ordinary life; they are at one end of a continuum between total engagement on the one hand and total detachment on the other. It is possible to use the word 'love' to apply to other forms of engagement with the other that are neither as complete nor as permanent. The injunction to love one's neighbour as oneself can be seen in this light, with a level of identification that runs from a simple acknowledgement of the other's existence, to a complete and ongoing support through life's crises. It is another mark of how detached our society has become that people living next door to each other can fail to recognize one another in the street.

Love implies mutuality and reciprocity. The natural community of the family all too often fails because it is founded on unequal relationships and any love it contains is an unhealthy, exploitative kind that entraps rather than liberates. Children often have to fight to get free, leaving a legacy of mutual distrust and antagonism. It is a mire in which many an experiment in community has foundered. True love allows people to move on and wishes them well. It implies mutuality, trust, respect, openness and a willingness to reveal oneself to the other that is a significant departure from the norms that have governed human relationships for the past few hundred years, at least in Western Europe. It is a way of approaching life based on accepting personal responsibility rather than a set of rules for conduct.

The concept of 'love' turns the balance between freedom and equality from an abstract debate into a living issue for each and every one of us. By exploring the boundaries between self and other within the context of a community of like-minded souls, we are more likely to discover our true natures, in which the clamour for self-gratification will be seen to be a superficial front disguising the vacuum beneath, a vacuum caused by the lack of true contact with others. Being able to meet real needs, having a sense of self-esteem and being part of something larger than one's self will also quieten the gnawing hunger to consume in order to prove that one exists.

A natural sense of sufficiency becomes a moral stance that reinforces a sense of personal responsibility. It creates the space that allows us to become more aware of the needs of others and of our environment in general. Freedom and equality may be the starting point in the adventure of community. Without love, however, it is an arid journey that ends in a desert of disillusion and despair. As with an arranged marriage, love can develop, but a loveless community imprisons its members and condemns them to a joyless existence of going through the motions.

In face-to-face contact with other human beings with whom we have a developing network of relationships, we are also more likely both to experience and to openly discuss the numinous. Although spiritual progress has often been linked to withdrawal from the world – the saint or hermit turning inwards to seek a new dimension – as the ultimate way of experiencing the merging of the self with the divine, for most of us increasing awareness of the immaterial world is likely to depend on having others around us who are interested in sharing all aspects of our existence.

Exploring sides of ourselves that may not have had much exposure allows the development of a new, mutual language, which may, in time, come to include elements of ritual, prayer, worship and praise (all of which are present in traditional religious observance). Through the evolution of this language, experience is both felt more deeply and set within a framework that allows it to be built upon and taken forward. Isolated experience is seen to be part of a wider pattern.

A community is also likely to develop a sense of continuity that is manifest in myths about its creation and its history. Tradition and rites of passage add to this sense of permanence and root the individual in time and place. Artistic expression, dreams (exploring reality through Jungian archetypes), visioning and spiritual experience all have important roles in developing and sustaining a sense of unique communal identity. To have contributed or shared something, however small, in this kind of social context offers a tangible legacy because it is more likely to have been acknowledged in the first place and to be reinforced, even years later, by other members of the community keeping it alive in their own memories.

This natural human desire to paint oneself on a wider canvas, to make one's mark, is fundamental to the development of a sense of who one is. Seeing the fruit of something you have been involved in all around you, every day, is a powerful acknowledgement of one's importance. One literally feels at home. In a community you can just be; in a corporation it is not unusual to have never been once you go out the door.

Clarity of language and strong social cohesion develop rapidly in the face of a challenge. They all too easily fall away into complacency and apathy when all is well and events happen predictably. People look back to the Second World War with nostalgia and longing because it offers a clear reference point in their lives and a sense of having been involved in something important. Both those are crucial factors in establishing the sense of integrity that seems to be one of the tasks of old age, the going back and making sense of one's life. This pursuit of integrity and authenticity requires the kind of significance, both for one's self and others, that a lifetime passing in and out of a series of large, anonymous institutions (the arena in which most of us make our contribution) will be hard-pressed to deliver.

A community does not just happen, and experience shows that it is incredibly difficult to create and sustain. While the countless community development officers employed by both statutory and voluntary agencies over the past 20 years may have contributed significantly to the ongoing debate about how to build community, it is a sad fact that, with a few notable exceptions, they have failed to deliver anything tangible or lasting. Looked at from the perspective of personal responsibility and consensus, there is some-thing faintly ludicrous about a person being paid to go into an area and attempt to create a sense of community. That is not to say that someone from outside may not be able to assist in the process, particularly if they have the requisite skills, but people have to want to come together sufficiently to be able then to achieve something together. There has to be a sense of identity and mere geography in a highly mobile age does not seem to be a sufficient motivating force.

How do we rediscover this sense of connectedness in a world that continues to fragment? A starting point is to look afresh at our networks of relationships (as local as possible) and view them as potential communities of interest. Plenty of nodes do exist around which varying degrees of com-munity might adhere. Adult education classes, local poli-tical parties, cafés, libraries, churches, groups of neighbours and interest groups all have the potential to harness the skills and energies of individuals in the cause of something larger than themselves. In the process of getting to know others who share an interest or way of looking at life, we are more likely to be able to exercise personal responsibility, allowing a form of natural community, based on mutual aid, to emerge. The exploration of personal responsibility and consensus within these contexts will also strengthen the social fabric and provide other opportunities for cooperation and experiment.

Another way of developing our networks of relationships in a way that might lead to community is to recognize that the little power we wield as individuals is expressed through consumption. That impact could be increased dramatically if we were to organize ourselves into groups to negotiate directly with suppliers and producers. Anything from electricity to organic vegetables could be purchased more cheaply, in ways that suit the consumer rather than the supplier, and at potentially better quality, through acting cooperatively. By building on personal contacts, whole neighbourhoods could be brought closer together by virtue of a shared interest in getting the best service at the cheapest cost.

Rather than seeing it in purely market terms, however, such initiatives offer the possibility of promoting decision-making arrangements that are more in keeping with the principles of personal responsibility, consensus and community than with a triumphalist neighbourhood plc. The growth of such structures will create wider horizons and might suggest that the next step is to look at the viability of creating the community's own electricity and growing its own quality food, all of which will increase its control over its own destiny.

Again, many embryonic examples of cooperative purchasing exist (neighbourhood coops, groups coming together to purchase and distribute organic food) and, in the wider economy, there is no doubt that consumer organizations wield real power. Once the possibilities inherent in purchasing goods and services cooperatively on a very local basis become more widely appreciated, many other initiatives will suggest themselves. From sharing tools and equipment in a planned way (operating a neighbourhood tool-hire service) to encouraging local industry (identifying individuals with skills such as making curtains and advertising their services locally), from neighbourhood workshops to cook and share schemes (people who enjoy cooking producing more than they need themselves, freezing the surplus, which can then be ordered by others in the scheme) can all provide the seed from which a community can grow.

THE WIDER PERSPECTIVE

No community can be an island. The question of the links between a community and the wider world raises two separate but related issues: how should communities coexist and what is the basis for trade between them?; is there a continuing need for some universal currency to handle transactions between communities, with all the dangers of it just being the existing, rapacious global economy by another name?

Although the clear advantage of basing social relations on local communities and local economies is that it represents the best chance of breaking our current addiction to private transport (with consequent major energy and pollution savings), we need to recognize that self-sufficiency at the community level is neither a desirable nor a realistic objective. Just as individuals are more likely to realize their potential by being interdependent with others (rather than dependent on or independent of them) so communities will benefit from ongoing ties with their neighbours.

Such interactions may result from individuals forming links with more than one community, through friendships or through trading (if you cannot find what you want within your own community, you will have to look elsewhere). In our current urban environments, for example, it is possible to envisage people trading primarily within their locality but having access to the resources of the entire city through some kind of 'yellow pages'.

Ultimately, however, there will be a need for formal systems of managing relationships between two (or more) communities. Decisions may have to be made about integrating communications systems such as roads; it might be appropriate to share some facilities and mutual aid might be required to tackle major projects. The same principles of personal responsibility, self-realization and consensus should inform these processes, and people with integrity will be needed to ensure that communities recognize each other's strengths and needs and respond accordingly.

Routine contact with neighbours will ensure that communities (no less than individuals) avoid the dangers of introspection and being unable to look at themselves in an honest and open light. Prejudice and complacency are less likely to take root and localities will become effectively self-managing as a consequence. In the same way that ongoing relations were maintained between the city states of ancient Greece through participation in regular festivals, games and religious rites, so communities might create opportunities to come together in enjoyable, relaxing contexts that not only allowed relationships between individuals and groups to develop over time, but began to forge a sense of local identity.

It is also possible to see how local, regional, continental and, ultimately, global structures might evolve along similar lines. Rather than being top-down and remote, however, each level will only deal with issues that cannot be resolved more locally (the meaning of that awkward word 'subsidiarity'!). The further removed from the issues facing real people and actual communities such bodies become, the greater the danger there is that participants will slip into discussing abstractions and end up trying to impose general solutions to complex problems. Once again, the quality of the individuals who are chosen to represent their communities, localities, and so on becomes paramount. Personal integrity, maturity, wisdom and the ability to embody the hopes and aspirations of others will be essential. Transparency will also be necessary to ensure that access to all relevant information is available.

Individuals demonstrating these characteristics are likely to be those who have realized their potential as communicators and facilitators and who are deeply versed in the workings of consensus and community. They are probably most appropriately chosen through consensus (rather than by election) and the more such individuals a community can call upon, the stronger it will be; representatives are only human and prolonged periods of acting in this capacity can dull the perception and lead to habitual, rather than creative, responses.

The aim is always to find ways forward that open up the potential for growth rather than to close it down. Paradoxical thinking, the ability to put oneself in another's shoes, to be in touch with one's whole self and what it is telling you, and an ability to live with uncertainty, will mark out those who have the skills to move things forward. They must never lose touch with their home community, however, and being a delegate must never become a full-time activity. To turn one's back on one's constituency is, in a very real sense, to lose touch with one's self, and only conceit and complacency can come from that. On the global

151

stage especially, humility and a realization of any individual's inadequacies in the face of such responsibility will be necessary to ensure that only appropriate decisions are taken.

To trade actively between communities, potentially across the globe, requires a medium of exchange. It is easy to see that two neighbouring communities that are both committed to basing their currency on an hour's work would have a stable, natural equivalence. Any transactions between the communities could be handled electronically, automatically crediting/debiting the participants in their own currency through community holding accounts that would have to be balanced occasionally, although it would be part of the ongoing negotiations between the communities to ensure that neither community became too indebted to the other – that is, became a net receiver of goods and services (which, again, might be viewed as getting rich at another's expense).

Trading further afield is more difficult. Firstly, such transactions are likely to be infrequent, Secondly, they may not be reciprocal (the providing community may want nothing that the purchasing community has to offer) and, finally, there are likely to be no mechanisms for direct negotiation about exchange rates. All these obstacles to open trading point to the ongoing need for overarching currencies covering whole regions – possibly a single, global currency – that would operate on the same values as a local currency – that is, making a profit would not be the principle on which it was founded.

As with individual trading, the onus would then be on the providing party to establish the purchaser's trading position. Are they in credit or commitment? How often do they trade? Is the proposed trade consistent with these patterns? What are their chances of balancing their universal account? Ethical trading considerations add other dimensions, such as a scrutiny of the quality of the community one is trading with. How firmly are they committed to the principles of freedom, equality and love? Are relationships with the local communities sound or is there evidence of unresolved conflict? Once again the principles of openness and transparency are crucial if personal responsibility is to be exercised effectively.

Trading between communities implies producing a surplus of commodities and services. What is to stop corporate-style structures emerging that are highly 'efficient' in terms of producing what people want over a wide geographical area, but which are effectively pursuing that interest at the expense of the communities in which they are rooted? Forms of organization reflect the dominant social relations in society. The current push towards globalization is merely the logical outcome of the kind of hierarchical, authoritarian decision-making structures that have evolved over the past 200 years, made possible by the communications revolution.

Localized communities would have very different priorities, expressed through a different set of social relations. There would be many safeguards to ensure that production reflected the desire to promote personal responsibility, consensus as well as community, and was firmly grounded in the principles of freedom, equality and love. As we have seen, the building of a factory would be fundamentally a community enterprise. One of the considerations in deciding to commit resources to such a scheme would undoubtedly be the potential market for the goods produced. A major factor might even be the opportunity to earn universal currency, both to pay for elements of the factory that had to be brought in from outside – for example, materials – and to allow the community to trade on a broader front.

But they could not override the basic humanity that is so entrenched in the process.

There are also reasons to suppose that large-scale systems simply would not work. To achieve wider sales, the community would have to enjoy some inherent advantages that would overcome the disadvantages of increasing transportation costs the further afield the exports went. Advantages might include access to natural resources, the particular skills/interests/knowledge available within the community (including improved technology, new techniques, and so on) and the position of competitors. One option not available would be to cut costs by paying less for the work element – that is, departing from the principle of an hour for an hour. Purchasers taking an ethical stance would prefer a product that honestly reflected the work that had gone into it, even if it cost more.

For the same reason, any technology employed would have to be demonstrably environmentally friendly and life-enhancing (in the sense that it did not deprive the people involved in the process of a sense of achievement or strip them of their skills). All these considerations suggest that goods travelling large distances will be penalized, and this limitation is likely to lead to a growth in the shipment of semi-finished products that can be completed to a customer's own requirements in a well-equipped local workshop. Machinery itself may become migratory, with several communities sharing access to specialized equipment.

Similarly, a group of communities may negotiate the way that production is allocated, allowing each to produce something different. It is important, however, to ensure that such agreements do not lead to complacency and a reluctance to face the need for change. Individuals and communities should always be able to challenge the status quo, and if that means existing arrangements failing or requiring radical overhaul, that is the price the organism has to pay to remain healthy; people or communities that find they can no longer compete (on the basis of the principles implicit in freedom, equality and love) will face a major re-evaluation of what they are about, a painful but ultimately growth-promoting opportunity.

Communities are organisms; they live, grow, divide and die, and mechanisms will have to be evolved to handle this natural progression. In practice, all systems have an in-built inertia and the number of times that the world has to be stood on its head will be few and far between. The question of how to avoid stagnation, complacency and apathy, however, must be addressed continually.

Once the idea that a community is a vibrant, living organism, with a set of life-giving processes to sustain it, takes hold of the imagination, one begins to see the social landscape through a different set of eyes. Thinking of a fishing port, for example, as a community sounds like history coming full circle. But the wheel, in turning, moves on and the crucial difference from the past is in the nature of the social relations between the members. By emphasizing relationships built on mutuality and reciprocity rather than on blood or position, there is a qualitative difference. For perhaps the first time in human history we face the possibility of being able to create the conditions where people can be truly themselves and live in communities that benefit from the whole-hearted contribution of all their members.

SUMMARY

The four dimensions – personal responsibility, consensus, local currencies and community – overlap and reinforce one another, but 'the greatest is community'. Community implies the presence of the other three, while the reverse is not so obviously true. It is perfectly possible to have a local currency that reflects the priorities of the money economy and, by implication, emphasizes the differentials in choice that the participants can exercise. Equally, personal responsibility can be exercised to a considerable degree in defined circumstances with very little direct relationship between the people involved.

All four dimensions nevertheless have to be present if we are to make progress and are in a constant state of creative imbalance. The bad news, therefore, is that we have to work on four fronts at once; the good news is that by concentrating on one we are likely to affect the others directly. In any given set of circumstances, the skill comes in choosing a strategy that will have maximum impact across the board. Introducing a local currency, for example, may get people trading but do little to increase the sense of community, because people might live too far apart to establish a common identity. A group might work to achieve consensus but have no real decision-making powers.

The starting point has to be ourselves and a recognition that things will have to change if the world is to be rebuilt. It begins a process that is very different from a desire to change the world. For a start, changing the world is a Herculean task and one that leads only to disillusion and frustration because it is beyond the capacity of any one individual to achieve. Paradoxically, it is also flawed for the simple reason that it assumes that we know best and it is for the rest of humanity to see things from our point of view; it is for them to change, not us.

We must *all* change and in ways that none of us can predict. The only stance that makes sense is to acknowledge that we are setting off on a personal journey and to concentrate on what we ourselves can realistically influence and change. We must begin by learning to accept personal responsibility.

For the reasons outlined above, that will not be easy. The opportunities for true personal exchange with others have become very limited. But if we are prepared to explore our own behaviour, beliefs and assumptions/prejudices honestly and openly by taking the time to understand another's point of view, we can begin to reclaim the human element in our lives. We will cease to treat people as objects and begin to grant them their own individual autonomy. Trust will creep into our relationships and change the way we relate to the wider world.

The more that mutual identification exists, the more likely we are to be willing to join with others in determining the issues that affect us all. Consensus is not about the sub-merging of self in a group; it is an opportunity to discover one's true self through participation in a process that engages the whole self and ends with an agreement that everyone can own, that has become part of each person's self. The more skilled people become at seeking consensus, the more readily it emerges.

Local currencies promote personal responsibility and consensus through the encouragement of trade between real, fully functioning human beings. It provides a context which emphasizes relationships as well as a framework in which each individual's skills can be recognized and valued. Genuine wealth is created, a wealth that reflects the priorities of the people involved rather than some imposed and ever-changing notion of what is fashionable. It is wealth that belongs to the community, rather than to some distant landlord or corporation, and thereby empowers and validates the holders in their negotiations with neigh-bouring and other communities.

157

True community is built on the bedrock of personal responsibility, a commitment to consensus and a willingness to participate fully in a local economy. It provides the individual with a context in which life becomes both meaningful and in which they can make a contribution. Past, present and future assume a coherence that assists in the individual task we all face of making sense of our lives, of achieving integrity.

Difference becomes something to be celebrated rather than feared and a community that manages to embrace a variety of skills and opinions is the stronger for it. It is yet another paradox that an individual is more likely to be free to be themselves within a community where uniqueness is valued and encouraged than in a world that is superficially tolerant of difference, but where public opinion can ride roughshod over individuals and groups who are caught momentarily in the spotlight of media attention because they *are* different in some way.

Taken together, these four strengths represent humanity's best chance of creating a sustainable future that offers the hope of a quality life for everyone. As such, they stand in stark contrast to the fragilities that are so evident in our current affairs and that, unless some significant changes occur, can only lead to everyone – young and old, rich and poor, male and female – being engulfed by catastrophe.

What have we got to lose in trying to change direction? Our precious dignity, perhaps; but people who laugh or cavil at us were never true friends, respecting us and trusting our integrity, prepared to give us the benefit of the doubt. By seeking to be part of a network of relationships built on freedom, equality and love, we may just discover that, far from being shut out in the cold, we have finally come home.

END PIECE

If I accept that it is my personal responsibility to move this agenda forward, then there are many levels on which I can begin the task. There is a certain aptness in starting with myself and in seeking out opportunities for personal growth and development, of finding more positive ways of dealing with the vicissitudes of life, and of relating to those closest to me in a more open and honest way. In more formal decision-making situations I can begin to reflect about consensus and, where appropriate, begin to actively encourage the expression of differing viewpoints. I can join (or seek to start) a local currency and I can become involved in community activities and attempt to raise their profile. The one option I don't have is to do nothing.

This 'bottom-up' approach is, in itself, unlikely to be enough, however. As noted earlier, we are part of a socially structured reality that will either help or hinder our attempts to improve the situation. At the very least, it will actively resist moves to fundamentally change its agenda. At the worst it will halt them in their tracks. There are enough examples of people facing jail for resisting arms sales, destroying genetically modified crops, and so on, to show that repression is never far away and that it does not take much to trigger it.

For the moment, we live in a quasi-democracy and we would do well to take advantage of the fact. There are a number of things that we can campaign for that would improve the chances of more fundamental changes occurring. And with each change in the status quo the next becomes easier still. The following suggestions of ways in which we might influence the government to promote 'community' are not intended to be comprehensive, nor are they in any order of priority. They will hopefully prompt ideas that individuals might wish to pursue for themselves.

- A commitment to halt, and preferably reverse, the slide into legislating for every aspect of life by encouraging a growth in 'mediation', the bringing together of the parties involved in disputes in an attempt to find a mutual way forward. At the very least, this option would be cheaper in the long run than the escalating cost in lawyers' fees.

- A commitment to placing the experiencing and exploring of human relationships (on an individual and group basis) at the very centre of our education system. This emphasis would ultimately change the nature of what goes on in our schools (where individuals are currently prepared for an individualistic, competitive and over-organized world that we are seeking to change).

- A commitment to ensuring that all government-funded initiatives (urban regeneration, health action, and so on) allocate resources for the facilitation of appropriate decision-making processes. There is still a tendency for such schemes to be imposed from above, leaving the people they are supposed to benefit unengaged and untouched. True regeneration is not a quick fix but a long-term building of new partnerships and alliances; the role of the outsider should be to facilitate this growth and create the conditions in which they are self-sustaining. There are clear implications for the training of people employed to work on such projects.

- A commitment to be mindful of natural communities in all decision-making processes. Just as we seek to protect endangered animal species, so government, at all levels, should do its best to ensure that vibrant, living communities are not driven to the wall by decisions that are made at a distance from them. We can always (and unfortunately will) build another superstore or motorway, but we cannot replace a community that has been destroyed in the process.

- A commitment to frame legislation that will encourage local initiatives towards economic self-sufficiency, including power generation and distribution, and so on.
- A commitment to removing any obstacles to the development of local currencies – for example, regulations relating to tax and social security.

Much can be achieved within a framework of a benign, if centralized, power structure. The credit union movement is a classic example, and in some countries – for example the Republic of Ireland – represents a major source of saving and borrowing that exists outside the money-making machine. Pushing back the boundaries, overcoming obstacles is the traditional, liberal way forward. And it works. But we should not delude ourselves that the institutional juggernaut is anything other than essentially anti-life and that it is capable of great damage to individuals. It is not going to be an easy journey, but each of us possesses the resources to emerge triumphant and to create a world where people and their communities really do matter.

A second area in which we can work to push the status quo in ways that will promote a sense of community is to experiment with the potential offered by the Internet. Major changes in social relationships have usually been preceded by technological innovation. The Industrial Revolution would have been impossible without innovative machinery and the sources of power to drive it. The capital required to start such ventures and the cut-throat nature of the marketplace determined a set of social relations that reflected the 'master's' investment and the factory conditions that the new processes required.

By contrast, the computer and the worldwide web that it provides access to is becoming generally available to all. For purely commercial reasons, governments want everyone to have access to the net. However, by emphasizing communication skills rather than brute strength, it provides an almost infinite range of ways of relating to one another (and thus a genuine opportunity to reverse the current imbalance between the masculine and feminine principles). It also allows us to be ourselves rather than forcing square pegs into round holes, which is the feature of most existing forms of social organization. All of which means that we have the potential to create more equitable social relationships than at any stage of human history. Whether we do is now largely down to us.

I know from my own experience that a sense of community can be sustained (for a limited period of time) over the net, and a recent televised experiment in Sunderland showed that providing Internet access to a very ordinary street did promote increased social interaction and a sense of community.[9] Young and old experimented enthusiastically, and the creation of the street's own website with a chat room and noticeboard allowed people to get to know each other more effectively than years of living next door to one another.

The worldwide web is altering language in front of our eyes. It is an opportunity, and we should do all we can to ensure that the resulting changes to the social fabric move us closer to the kind of sustainable communities that this book has been exploring.

Focusing the Mind

The millennium is an arbitrary date, having no more importance than any other point in time. As individuals, however, we crave significance and seek to tie it down through language. One of the most significant aspects of our human existence is the passage of time and, with it, the inevitable shortening of our own mortal span. It is something we cannot escape and, to cope, we break time up, thereby fooling ourselves that we have come to control it. In the process we create a series of milestones along the way.

For each of us our birthday is a reminder that another year has passed. Some anniversaries are given more weight than others. A fiftieth, for example, is traditionally a time to begin to take stock and to prepare oneself for whatever portion remains. It is a psychological mechanism for coming to terms with the changes that inevitably accompany ageing.

So it is with the millennium. Human history consists of periods and ages (linked to individuals and dynasties) and the turning of centuries has provided a natural opportunity for renewal, a refocusing of energy and a redefinition of what it means to be human. Millennia are centuries writ large, an almost mandatory requirement to pause for thought. We know that many in the West believed that AD1000 would mark the end of the world. The survival of the species – or at least that element of it that resided in Christendom, the date having passed unnoticed throughout the rest of the planet – produced an explosion of church and cathedral building that lasted over 200 years and left a testament to hidden truths that we can only marvel at.

Five hundred years later and western civilization was in the midst of the flowering of the Renaissance – another outpouring of the human spirit – whose concern with the individual and with demonstrable truth still reverberates around the world today. Is it too far-fetched to suggest that the next century will see change on no less dramatic a scale?

This manifesto suggests that the most hopeful way in which that change might find expression is through an increasing understanding of ourselves and of our relationships with others. It does not underestimate the difficulties in switching from the path we currently seem doomed to follow, but it does suggest that such change is possible. Like a heavily laden freight train that screams across the points as it switches tracks, before thundering on as if nothing had happened, it is that initial change of direction that is the most challenging, confusing and frightening. The choice is ours, to continue to be swept along by forces over which we have little control (to accept our fate passively) or to begin to take control of our destinies by grounding our actions on the bedrock of an increasing awareness of who we are and what is important in our lives.

We have thrown off the arbitrary ties and obligations of feudalism and patriarchy only to find ourselves adrift on a sea of anonymity and prey to any passing hazard. To re-establish a more healthy balance between vulnerability and safety, we need to develop networks of relationships based on mutuality and respect, where rights and responsibilities are freely given and accepted. Implicit in the idea of community (which, in turn, embraces personal responsibility, consensus and local currencies) is a movement towards small-scale communities that meet their own needs as far as possible, while coexisting with their neighbours – and, ultimately, the global community – on the same principles.

The emphasis will be truly on the individual, but incorporate a concept of individuality that is anchored firmly in a force-field of mutual support and shared perceptions of what is important in life. No longer will people feel and act like isolated atoms in a hostile universe, facing the prospect of being overwhelmed by forces over which they have no control. An environment will have been created in which we can each achieve our potential as unique individuals, an environment in which the quality of our relationships with those around us will be a measure of just how far we have moved towards self-realization.

Such communities will comprise individuals who are at peace with themselves, their neighbours, their environment and whatever meaning they might discover for their existence. It is a dream, of course, but is it not better to have dreamed, and only partially realized that dream, than never to have dreamed at all? We all need to have a sense of direction, and what better than one that believes it is possible to build a better world?

Where's the catch? There is no one to tell us what we can or cannot do. We do not need a qualification to exercise personal responsibility, there is not a European Standard to measure community, and no one is going to come and inspect our local currency and write us off as failing. It's down to each one of us to set off on the journey. And that is the problem. We lack imagination, we prefer the familiar and we are lazy. It is actually easier to accept that we have to do things the way they are, even if doing them is not good for our health, than to consciously take responsibility for changing the way we live. We have accepted our fate rather than being prepared to create it.

If change is to happen, however, it is going to require a significant number of people being prepared to take that first step (many already have, but the critical mass is still a long way off). We cannot sit around waiting for the government to pass laws that say that the country should be parcelled up into community-sized chunks – whatever they might be – and each should start local currencies. Even if such an unlikely step were to occur, it would be institutional in nature and merely a continuation of what is in another guise.

Government can certainly assist the process and may eventually follow the lead given by its citizens by giving formal approval to developments that have already taken place, but it is we as individuals who have to break new ground. The canvas is all but blank and we are going to have to fill in the detail. That is both a scary and liberating thought. The good news is that we can start today.

Of course, there is an alternative. The scenario painted in the first section – in which the global economy lurches from crisis to crisis before finally melting down completely – may determine the nature of existence for most of us in the foreseeable future. Survival may become the name of the game and any notion of autonomous communities living at peace with their neighbours will come to seem absurdly idealistic.

The strength of the thinking behind the concept of such communities, however, is precisely that it offers both a vision for a sustainable future and our best hope for avoiding the arbitrary ravages of the large-scale, institutional world. Precisely because it does have a measure of independence from external forces, a community with a strong local economy and clear ideas about the importance of people is the best bulwark against the unpredictable responses of both global markets and distant hierarchies.

If a crash does come, the unprotected individual will almost certainly be left out in the cold.

Many groups are gearing themselves up for precisely such an eventuality, but digging in for long-term survival can produce a bunker mentality that is almost as dehumanizing – paranoid, penny-pinching and lacking in joy – as the culture it is seeking to protect itself from. Far better is an attitude that acknowledges the dangers inherent in the status quo but sees community as a positive alternative that is worth working towards for its own sake.

The energies released in attempting to explore the possibilities inherent in a new world view are likely to be more creative and life-affirming than those produced in a last-ditch attempt to shore up the defences against catastrophe. If existing structures do collapse before viable alternatives are in place, however, a basis for survival will exist and provide a framework within which people can retrench and make the best of whatever situation they find themselves in.

It feels as if we are on a cusp of history. There is a sea-change in the air and, while it is important that we do not minimize the dangers, it is even more crucial to hold on to the idea that anything can be achieved if there is sufficient belief. Every age is a crossroads with multiple choices but, for ours, the consequences of getting it wrong seem starker than most.

The same is true of individuals. We all face choices at every step of the way. The easiest course is always to go with the flow, to allow oneself to be carried along in the mainstream. The alternative, to step aside, to throw off the familiar and begin a journey that will take us into the unknown, is always difficult. It requires courage, but each second we delay only makes the ultimate decision even harder. To recognize that we are on a ship that will one day founder may help and, to extend the analogy, it is natural to want to stay on board until the signs of trouble can no longer be ignored. The danger is that we will leave it too late and be dragged down as the stricken vessel makes its final plunge.

Abandoning ship is a once-and-for-all decision and it is perhaps more practical to think in terms of planning our departure, taking advantage of fine days and calm seas to experiment with alternatives, seeking the familiar at first and gradually venturing deeper into unknown territory. One day we might look back and find that we have all but left our previous dependencies behind. We will have found a lifeboat and be ready to strike out for a new homeland.

There is endless scope for experimentation and it is important not to be discouraged by apparent failure. For every five local currencies being set up at the moment, for example, only one or two will really take off. In each of our own lives there are times when we are receptive to change and others when we are likely to dig our heels in and resist. So it is with groups of people presented with the chance to break new ground. The time has to be right and no amount of effort will move things on if the participants are not yet ready. But tomorrow is another day, and what seemed hard only yesterday is taken in our stride and we hardly notice. The only crime is to do nothing. By concentrating on taking the first step, the next will suggest itself.

There is a new world out there waiting to be claimed. We are not talking of abandoning our civilization. It has done perhaps more than any other to raise our perceptions of what we as humans can aspire to, but it is now no longer in ours, or anybody's, control. The time has come to salvage what is good and strike out afresh, confident that the world view we have inherited does contain its share of truth and can provide a beacon to guide us in the darkest hours.

There comes a point in the affairs of humanity when the thinking and talking have to stop, when it is time to get on with what needs to be done. That time has come.

Notes and References

INTRODUCTION

1 Miller, A (1990) 'The American Clock' in *Plays Three*, Methuen Drama, London, p45

A THOROUGHLY MODERN WAY OF LIVING

1 Lietaer, B (1998) 'The Future of Money – From Global to Local Currencies', Keynote speech delivered at *The LETSLINK UK Complementary Currencies Conference*, Portsmouth, 16 October
2 Robertson, J (1998) 'Our Money', *New Internationalist*, no 306
3 'The Facts of Money' (1998), *New Internationalist*, no 306
4 Ibid
5 Douthwaite, R (1996) *'Short Circuit – Strengthening Local Economies for Security in an Unstable World'*, Green Books, Totnes
6 Ferguson, N (1998) *The Pity of War*, Allen Lane, Penguin Press, London
7 Orwell, G (1949) *Nineteen Eighty-Four*, Penguin Books, Harmondsworth
8 See, for example, entry under 'Petroleum' (1994), on *Encarta*, Microsoft Corporation
9 Toffler, A (1973) *Future Shock*, Pan Books, London

10 'Universal Declaration of Human Rights' (1948), adopted by The General Assembly of the United Nations on 10 December
11 Neimoeller, M (1968), in *Congressional Records*, 12 October

WAYS OF THE WORLD

1 Erikson, E H (1974) *Childhood and Society*, Pelican Books, Harmondsworth, Chapter 7
2 Ibid, p259
3 Sexton, S (1999) *Food? Health? Genetic Engineering and World Hunger*, The Corner House, Dorset
4 Suzuki, D (1998) quoted in an article in *Higher Guardian*, 3 December
5 Liedloff, J (1986) *The Continuum Concept*, Penguin Books, Harmondsworth
6 See, for example, Milgram, S (1974) *Obedience to Authority*, Harper & Row, New York
7 Mulgan, G (1998), *Connexity*, Vintage, London
8 Sanderson, C (1993) 'Chernobyl – Out of Darkness', in *Townsend Letter*, an informal letter magazine for doctors communicating with doctors, August/September

REGAINING A SENSE OF DIRECTION

1 Harlow, J (1999) 'Middle Classes Give Up On Friends', *The Sunday Times*, 18 May
2 Tannen, D (1998) *The Argument Culture*, Virago Press, London
3 Belbin, M, papers of the Industrial Training Research Unit, Cambridge

4 The Institute of Cultural Affairs (ICA) is a global network of private, non-profit, non-governmental organizations. Autonomous national ICAs operate in 34 countries worldwide, federated in the Institute of Cultural Affairs International (ICAI) which is based at The Institute of Cultural Affairs, rue Amédéé Lynen 8, B-1210 Brussels, Belgium; email icauk@gn.apc.org

5 The Foundation for Community Encouragement was formed to explore the insights into community building contained in the works of M Scott Peck – for example, *The Different Drum*. Its US headquarters is based at PO Box 449, Ridgefield, CT 06877. A UK offshoot, Community Building in Britain (CBiB), is contactable via 1 Evergreen Close, Woolmer Green, Herts, SG3 6JN; email PeterCBIB@aol.com

6 The New Economics Foundation (NEF) is a charity working to construct a new economy centred on people and the environment. They are based at Cinnamon House, 6–8 Cole Street, London, SE1 4YH; telephone 020 7407 7447; website: www.neweconomics.org. Environmental Resolve is an undertaking of The Environment Council and is a leading environmental mediation service in the UK, helping to prevent environmental disputes by using consensus-building processes. They are based at The Environment Council, 212 High Holborn, London, WC1V 7VW; telephone 020 7836 2626; website: www.the-environment-council.org.uk. Mediation Ltd is a national charity representing and supporting mediation within local communities. Contact details and more information can be found by accessing their website at www.mediationuk.org.uk; telephone 0117 904 6661

7 Mitchell Waldrop, M (1996) *The Trillion-Dollar Vision of Dee Hock*, first appeared in Fast Company, October/November, p75

8 Wright, C (1997), *The Sufficient Community*, Green Books, Totnes
9 *Dispatches* 'Gayhurst Crescent Goes Surfing' (2000) on Channel 4 Television, 2 March

Index

adversarial approach 53,
111–112, 114, 124
agribusiness 13–20, 38, 67,
142
architecture 50
archetypes 64
Arkwright, Richard 95
Armageddon 3
Asia 36
Austen, Jane 47
authority 114, 116, 123

balance 22, 55, 70, 83–84,
87, 88, 92, 93, 107, 117,
122, 130, 132, 142, 144,
156
banking 10, 20
Boyle's Law 84
BSE 18, 28
bureaucracy 20, 21, 22, 72,
86, 101, 109

Chernobyl 88
children/childhood 52,
78–80, 143, 144
civilization 1–4, 12, 18, 20,
38, 39, 43, 67, 73, 168

collective unconscious 64
command-and-control
decision making
20–28, 38, 142
Common Agricultural
Policy 14, 19
community 11, 44, 59–60,
82, 85, 88–89, 93, 107,
118, 127, 128, 134, 137,
138, 139, 137, 139, 140,
141–155, 157, 158, 159,
160, 161, 165, 166
consensus 109–125, 127,
128, 132, 136, 141, 143,
147, 148, 150, 151,
156–157, 158, 164
consultation 115, 122
consumer rights 24
contract 101, 102
covenant 101–102, 117
credit 135, 152
credit unions 161
culture 2, 48, 56, 70, 71, 90
currency markets 6, 7, 8
cyberspace 23

Darby, Abraham 95

Darwin, Charles 47, 66
decision making 91, 93, 99, 109, 110, 114–116, 132, 148
debt 10, 11, 14, 135, 138, 139, 152
democracy 8, 96, 142, 159
Descartes, René 54
developing world 11, 19, 68–69
divorce 32

ecology 83
economic growth 70
education 20, 27, 79, 101, 160
Egypt 47
Einstein, Albert 47
employment 129
employment law 25
Enlightenment, the 28, 55, 57
equal opportunities 24
equality 141, 142, 143, 153, 158
Erikson, Erik 59
ethical trading 10
euro 7, 9, 137
evil 59, 84
evolution 65, 66, 73, 75, 78, 80
experts 31, 34, 108

fairy tales 49

faith 48, 65, 73–74, 77, 92, 93
faith healing 87–88
farming 13, 14, 16, 17, 19, 48, 112
fashion 50
fate 60, 61, 62, 94, 164, 165
feminine principle 70, 71, 87, 103, 108, 111, 162
feudalism 35, 164
feuds 31, 63
fields of force 43, 50, 52, 59, 118, 144, 165
First World War 11
fossil fuels 18, 19
freedom 35, 141, 142, 143, 153, 158
French Revolution 55
Freud, Sigmund 54, 57, 61, 62, 66

George, Eddie 9
genetics 35, 58, 65–69, 73, 74
global money econmy 6–12, 26, 69, 94, 126, 131, 133, 138, 142, 153, 166
government 95, 109, 113, 159, 160, 166
Great Depression, the 1, 12
Greece, Ancient 150

health 20, 27, 46, 67, 72, 82, 88

health and safety at work 24

Hitler, Adolf 36

Hobbes, Thomas 54

housing associations 137

human development 57, 58–59

human rights 29

humour 61

individual 28–35, 44, 59, 76, 82, 93, 106, 107, 120, 137, 141, 142, 147, 158, 163, 165

Industrial Revolution 95, 96, 112, 161

interest rates 8

International Monetary Fund 8

Ithaca hours 134

Japan 12

Jung, Carl 64

justice 84, 85

Justices of the Peace 32

Korean War 12

language 41–54, 56, 58, 65, 67, 72, 77, 86, 89, 90–94, 96, 97, 104, 113, 118, 142, 145, 146, 162

law 20, 24–26, 28–34, 37, 95, 103–104, 113–114, 160

LETS 134–135

local authorities 137

local economies 125–146, 156, 157, 159, 164, 166, 168

love 102, 131, 143–145, 157, 158

Marx, Karl 9

masculine principle 70, 71, 87, 103, 108, 111, 162

materialism 72, 8687, 92

maturity 52

Morris, William 125, 130

Mother Theresa 58

murder 32

Newton, Isaac 47, 55

North Vietnam 3

nuclear industry 68

Oedipus 62

organic farming 15,

paradox 44, 72, 75, 87, 92, 103, 116, 151, 158

participation 115, 122

patriarchy 35

personal responsibility 98–108, 116, 117, 118, 127, 128, 131, 141, 144, 145, 147, 148, 150, 156, 157, 158, 159, 164

polarization 70, 87

police 33
pollution 29
Pompeii 3
profit 37, 69, 133, 137, 152
public opinion 36, 113
Public Sector Borowing 8

quantum mechanics 68

Reformation 8
relationships 33, 81–83, 85,
    93, 100, 104, 108, 127,
    128, 141, 145, 147, 148,
    150, 158, 160, 164, 165
religion 73, 88, 146
Renaissance 164
Republic of Ireland 161
Rogers, Carl 57
Roman Catholic Church 7,
    8, 72
Roman Empire 3
Romantics 131
Romas 134
Rousseau, Jean Jacques 28,
    55
Russia 20, 36, 87

science 45, 46, 49, 50, 69, 70,
    72, 74, 92
scientific viewpoint 42,
    65–70, 92, 123, 125
Second World War 12, 59,
    68, 146

self-realization 58, 59, 66,
    91, 130, 131, 137, 143,
    150, 165
self sustaining agriculture
    17, 68
Shakespeare, William 58
Smith, Adam 95
Social Security 21, 30
Sparta 55
spirituality 42, 86–88,
    145–146
Sweden 11

taxation 8, 136
technology 15, 16, 109, 154,
    161
television 34, 53, 142
therapy 50, 59
Time Dollars 134
transparency 135, 153

uncertainty 83, 86, 92
unconscious 43, 60–64
United States 3, 7, 109

Victorian Britain 3

Weber, Max 22
Wordsworth, William 45
work 79, 80, 129, 130139
World Wide Web 29, 161,
    134, 162